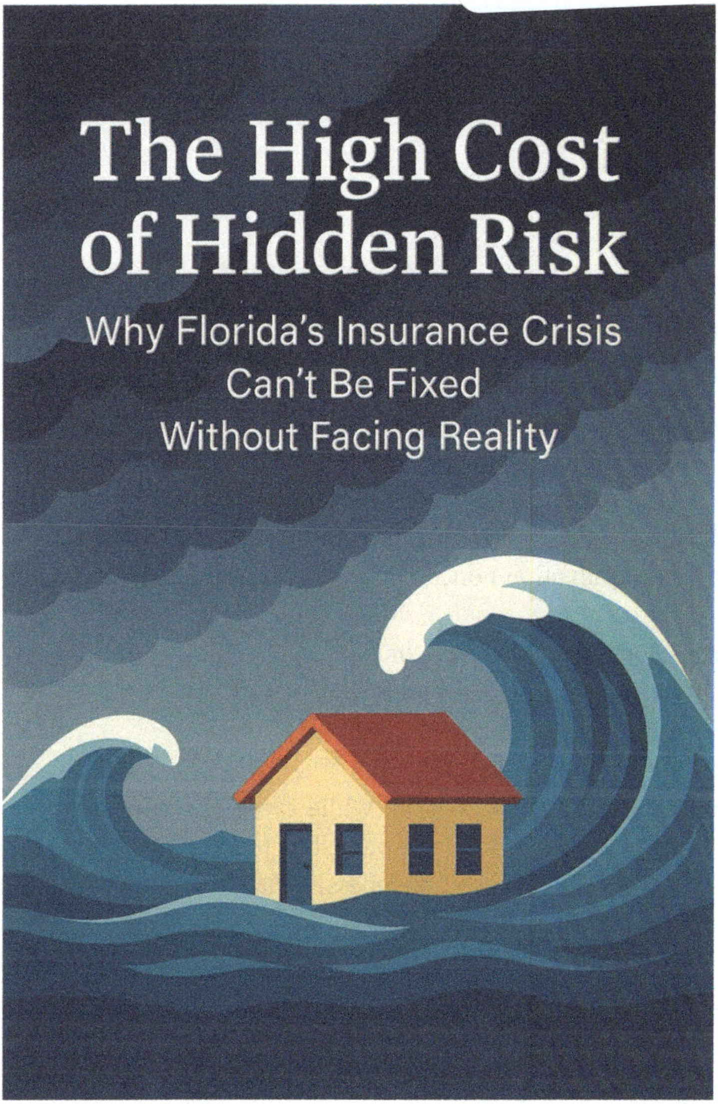

By: Don D. Brown

2025

Copyright Page

Published by Rebell Books
Atlanta, GA
ISBN: 978-1-967567-75-1

For permission requests, please contact:
Don D. Brown
don@dondbrown.com

Library of Congress Cataloging-in-Publication Data:
[Placeholder for Cataloging Information, if applicable]

Cover design by Don D. Brown
Printed in the United States of America
First Edition: 2025

Table of Contents

The High Cost of Hidden Risk: Why Florida's Insurance Crisis Can't Be Fixed Without Facing Reality

Prologue: The Executive Warning

What if Florida's greatest financial risk isn't hurricanes themselves, but how we insist on paying for them?

For decades, leaders have promised homeowners that coverage can be both cheap and sufficient. They said we could outwit geography, ignore probability, and tame catastrophe with the stroke of a legislative pen. It was a soothing promise — like believing you can live on credit forever without ever facing the bill. But storms don't wait for politics, and neither do financial obligations.

Florida is a peninsula that juts into the warmest waters of the Atlantic and the Gulf. Nearly half of all U.S. hurricanes make landfall here. Catastrophe is not an aberration — it is our baseline. And yet, policy after policy has been built on the fiction that we can suppress prices, delay costs, and somehow come out ahead.

Every storm leaves a bill. The only real question is whether we pay it up front, with discipline and capital, or afterward, with debt and regret.

The Credit Card Illusion

Once upon a time, in a quiet Florida suburb, I lived next to Mr. and Mrs. Jones — the very embodiment of the American dream. Every evening, without fail, the Joneses would back their luxury SUV out of the driveway, announce their plans to enjoy another fine dining experience, and drive off with a sense of carefree indulgence. Their nightly ritual became the talk of the neighborhood — and the quiet envy of many.

One day, my wife turned to me and asked with a wry smile, "Why don't we ever go out to eat like the Joneses?"

I gave her the only answer a practical man could: "Because the Joneses are probably eating on credit."

But temptation is a powerful thing. And soon enough, I found myself applying for a high-limit credit card — not out of financial necessity, but to keep up with the illusion of prosperity. For months, we dined like royalty, charged every meal, and paid only the minimum balance. It was glamorous... until the bill came due.

By year's end, our card was maxed out, our finances were underwater, and all we had to show for our extravagant spending was a bloated waistline and an empty wallet. The meals were gone — flushed away — but the debt remained.

This simple parable reflects a larger, more dangerous story playing out across Florida's property insurance market. For decades, Florida has tried to "keep up with the Joneses" of affordability — suppressing insurance premiums through artificial pricing schemes, political pressure, and short-term policy fixes. The result has been a deceptive illusion of affordability… funded by credit, assessments, and future losses.[1]

Artificially low premiums feel good in the moment, but like dining on credit, the pleasure fades while the debt endures.

The Hidden Cost of "Cheap"

When politicians force premiums below actuarial reality, insurers exit the market. When state-backed entities like Citizens Property Insurance grow to fill the gap, they create enormous public liabilities. When catastrophe strikes, the state borrows billions, saddling every policyholder — from renters in Pensacola to business owners in Miami — with surcharges that linger for a decade or more.

We call this "affordability." In reality, it is a shell game. High-risk coastal homeowners are subsidized by inland families who may never see a storm surge. Current voters enjoy suppressed premiums while future generations inherit 30-year bonds for disasters they didn't cause. The system is not just inefficient — it is unjust.

A Choice Between Capital and Crisis

There are only two ways to fund catastrophe:

---

[1] Florida Office of Insurance Regulation (OIR), "Report on the Review of Florida's Residential Property Insurance Market," 2021. See also: Insurance Information Institute (III), "Florida's P&C Insurance Crisis: Causes and Consequences," 2022.

- **Pre-event funding** — saving in advance through premiums, reinsurance, catastrophe bonds, and mitigation investments.
- **Post-event funding** — borrowing afterward, taxing broadly, and disguising the cost through assessments.

History has shown the difference clearly. After Hurricane Wilma in 2005, Florida borrowed billions. Policyholders were still paying those assessments a decade later. By contrast, when Citizens issued catastrophe bonds in 2012, the capital was secured up front. The funds were available immediately if disaster struck, and no long-term debt burden fell on future policyholders.

The lesson is simple: capital-before-crisis is cheaper, faster, and more just.

Why This Book Matters

This book is not about abstract finance. It is about whether Florida families will be able to afford homes, businesses, and communities in the decades ahead. It is about whether we will continue chasing the illusion of affordability — or confront the reality that you cannot reduce premiums until you reduce losses, and you cannot reduce losses until you stop building in ways and places that guarantee catastrophe.

It is also about fairness. Should low-income families in inland Florida be taxed for decades to subsidize waterfront construction they could never afford? Should future generations be forced to repay bonds for storms that happened before they were born? Should political convenience dictate whether homes are hardened, roofs strapped, and communities made safe?

These are not technical questions. They are moral ones.

A Call to Principle

Florida's property insurance crisis is not simply an economic challenge — it is a test of political will, public understanding, and personal responsibility. We can continue to delay the bill, or we can start paying it honestly. We can continue to borrow against our future, or we can build a market that reflects reality and rewards resilience.

The storms will come. The bill will follow. The question is whether we will be ready — or still pretending we can afford not to be.

This book is my argument for readiness, for principle over politics, and for honesty over illusion. It is not about fear — it is about courage. The courage to acknowledge risk, the discipline to price it, and the vision to confront it before it destroys us.

When the next storm arrives — and it will — may no one say, "We didn't see this coming."

Part I

Chapter 1: Executive Summary

Florida's property insurance market has faced unprecedented stress over the past decade, marked by rising premiums, insurer insolvencies, and growing public concern. In response, the Florida Legislature enacted significant legal reforms in 2022 and 2023 aimed at curbing runaway litigation and restoring stability to the market. These reforms are beginning to yield positive effects, particularly in slowing the rate of market deterioration and improving insurer confidence.[2]

However, it should not be assumed that these legal remedies alone will result in dramatically lower premiums. The underlying driver of Florida's insurance crisis remains: catastrophic hurricane exposure amplified by human behavior that places people and property directly in harm's way.[3] Legal reform addresses the legal cost structure — not the physical risk itself.

This book argues that the only sustainable path forward is to **stop treating insurance pricing as a political problem and start confronting catastrophe risk as a structural one**. At the core of this thesis is a straightforward but often ignored truth:

---

[2] Florida Senate Bill 2A (2022) and Senate Bill 7052 (2023) addressed issues such as assignment of benefits (AOB), one-way attorney fees, and barriers to market entry, leading to early signs of market stabilization. See Florida Senate, 2022 Special Session A Summary: https://www.flsenate.gov.

[3] Florida has the highest hurricane landfall frequency in the U.S. (41%), and over 75% of its population lives in coastal counties. See NOAA National Hurricane Center, "Historical Hurricane Tracks," and U.S. Census Bureau, Coastal Population Report (2020).

Pre-funding catastrophe risk through capital reserves, reinsurance, and mitigation is both more economically efficient and socially responsible than post-event recovery financed through debt.[4]

In other words, paying for hurricanes before they happen is cheaper — and fairer — than paying for them afterward with borrowed money and financial pain disguised as policy relief.

The roots of Florida's insurance turmoil lie in three interlocking realities:

1. Catastrophic exposure to hurricanes, driven by geography and climate;5
2. Widespread vulnerability, exacerbated by building in high-risk coastal zones;6
3. Public policy that subsidizes or conceals risk, encouraging behavior that compounds future losses.7

This book provides a detailed examination of the market distortions created by policies such as HB1A (2007), which artificially suppressed rates and undermined market discipline.[8] It explores how deferred risk leads to post-event assessments, long-

---

[4] Congressional Budget Office (CBO), "Expected Costs of Damage from Hurricane Winds and Flooding," April 2022; see also GAO, "Disaster Resilience: Better Planning Needed to Manage Post-Disaster Funding," GAO-20-46.

[5] NOAA Hurricane Research Division, "Tropical Cyclone Landfall Statistics," accessed 2023; confirms Florida's high exposure to landfalling storms.

[6] FEMA and National Institute of Building Sciences, "Natural Hazard Mitigation Saves: 2019 Report," which details how much of Florida's housing stock is built pre-2002 and lacks wind mitigation features.

[7] Insurance Information Institute (III), "Understanding Moral Hazard in Public Insurance Systems," 2021; explains how misaligned incentives lead to increased public exposure.

[8] Florida House of Representatives, Bill Summary for HB1A (2007 Special Session); also see Florida Office of Insurance Regulation, Historical Rate Filing Reports.

term debt obligations, and cascading insurer insolvencies that ultimately punish the very homeowners these policies aim to protect.

Drawing on case studies, economic analysis, and public policy models from other catastrophe-prone regions, the paper proposes a principle-based framework built on transparency, accountability, and resilience. It advocates for risk-reflective pricing, pre-event capital investment, and targeted mitigation incentives that prioritize long-term affordability over short-term political relief.

In the end, the message is simple but essential:

We can't reduce insurance premiums until we reduce the losses. And we can't reduce the losses until we stop building in ways and places that guarantee catastrophe.

This is not merely an insurance problem. It is a test of political will, public understanding, and economic discipline. We face a choice between **storm defense and storm debt**. One path builds security. The other borrows against our future.

Chapter 2: Introduction – The Illusion of Affordability

Everyone loves a bargain. A discount on groceries, a sale at the car lot, a reduced premium on your home insurance. But not all bargains are real. Sometimes the price is lower only because the true cost has been hidden — shifted into the future, buried in fine print, or quietly assigned to someone else.

Florida's homeowners have lived under that illusion for decades. Politicians, under pressure from voters, have treated insurance premiums as a political problem rather than a financial reality. When rates rise, the temptation is irresistible: promise relief, cap premiums, or expand state-backed coverage. The result feels like a discount — but it is really a bill deferred.

This chapter explores how Florida mistook "cheap" insurance for real affordability, why those choices distorted the market, and how the consequences became unavoidable.

The Mirage of Cheap Rates

For much of the modern era, Florida has been locked in a cycle of denial. Each hurricane season brings losses, and each round of losses is followed by political intervention to "keep insurance affordable." The problem is not unique to Florida. Around the world, governments fall into the same trap — suppressing prices in the name of short-term relief, while planting the seeds of long-term instability.

But in Florida the trap is especially dangerous. Here, catastrophe risk is not an occasional threat but a constant.

Suppressing premiums does not erase that risk. It only hides the cost in other places: insurer insolvencies, surcharges on unsuspecting policyholders, and taxpayer-backed debt that lingers long after the storms pass.

The illusion works because it is immediate. The harm is delayed. And in politics, the delayed consequence is too often someone else's problem.

A Human Story: Maria's Surprise Bill

Consider Maria, a middle school teacher in Miami. In 2010, her premiums were modest, thanks in part to frozen Citizens Property Insurance rates. She could afford her home comfortably. But when her insurer failed after a storm season, Maria suddenly found herself paying more — not only higher premiums with a new company, but also hidden surcharges that appeared on her bill to cover past failures.

Maria hadn't done anything wrong. She hadn't moved, she hadn't filed a claim, she hadn't even upgraded her house. Yet she was paying more because the "cheap" rates of yesterday had been financed with the credit of tomorrow.

Maria's story is not unique. Hundreds of thousands of Floridians have discovered that what looks like short-term relief eventually arrives as long-term pain.

Illusions Beyond Florida

The pattern is universal. Around the globe, "affordability" is often achieved by hiding cost:

- Governments that subsidize fuel prices see shortages when demand surges beyond supply.
- Pension systems that promise benefits without adequate funding collapse under demographic strain.
- Health care programs that underprice coverage eventually ration care or shift costs to taxpayers.

Each case follows the same principle: when the true cost of risk is hidden, the eventual reckoning is larger and harsher.

Florida's insurance crisis belongs to that family of illusions. Like an underfunded pension or a subsidized fuel program, it looked generous in the moment but cruel in the aftermath.

The Cost of Denial

High premiums are not the problem. They are the price of the problem. When Florida hides that truth, homeowners don't make safer choices, developers keep building in risky zones, and policymakers avoid hard conversations.

The illusion of affordability doesn't just distort the market — it distorts behavior. And distorted behavior creates a feedback loop of vulnerability: more homes in high-risk areas, more damage from storms, more pressure to suppress rates again, and more insolvencies to follow.

The circle repeats, each time with higher stakes.

Looking Ahead

This chapter has introduced the central paradox of Florida's property insurance crisis: what looks like compassion in the short term becomes cruelty in the long term. The illusion of affordability is seductive, but it is unsustainable.

In the next chapter, we will shift from the mirage to the mechanics. We will explore the financial reality that every storm leaves a bill — and why paying with capital before disaster strikes is always cheaper, faster, and fairer than borrowing afterward.

Chapter 3: The Core Thesis – Capital Before Crisis

Every storm leaves a bill. The only real choice is whether we pay it before the damage, with discipline and capital, or afterward, with debt and regret.

There are only two funding models for catastrophe:

1. **Pre-event funding** — saving in advance through premiums, reinsurance, catastrophe bonds, and investments in mitigation.
2. **Post-event funding** — borrowing after the storm, taxing broadly, and disguising the true cost through assessments and state-backed debt.

Florida has tried both. The results are not in dispute: pre-event capital is cheaper, faster, and fairer. Post-event borrowing, by contrast, shifts the burden to people who never agreed to carry it — inland families, renters, and even future generations.

This is the financial core of Florida's insurance crisis. The illusion of affordability described in the last chapter works only because the state has repeatedly chosen to finance risk after the fact rather than price it honestly before disaster strikes. But as we will see, this is like buying flood insurance while the water is already rising — too little, too late, and far too expensive.

Capital or Debt: The Fork in the Road

When catastrophe strikes, the bill is immediate. Claims must be paid, homes rebuilt, and lives restored. The question is not whether the money will be spent but where it will come from.

- **Capital-first systems** collect premiums, purchase reinsurance, and issue catastrophe bonds before disaster. When the storm arrives, funds are available instantly, and the financial system remains stable.
- **Debt-first systems** rely on post-event borrowing. The state issues bonds, imposes assessments on all policyholders, and repays the debt over decades. The costs are spread widely but unfairly, often falling hardest on those least responsible for the losses.

Florida has leaned too often on the second model, creating a fragile market that depends on luck and low storm activity.

The True Cost of Borrowing

After Hurricane Wilma in 2005, Florida turned to debt to cover billions in losses. Policyholders across the state — even those hundreds of miles from landfall — received assessments on their policies for years. The storm had long passed, roofs had been repaired, and memories had faded. But the financial burden lingered.

By contrast, in 2012 Citizens Property Insurance issued catastrophe bonds to secure billions in capital before storm season. That money was available on day one if disaster struck, and repayment was limited to investors who had agreed to bear the risk. No broad-based assessments were required.

The contrast is clear: one system borrows from everyone without consent; the other attracts capital from those who willingly take risk in exchange for return.

Why Pre-Event Funding Works

Pre-event capital has three undeniable advantages:

1. **Speed** — Funds are available immediately when disaster strikes, without waiting for legislative action or bond sales.
2. **Cost** — Capital secured in advance is far cheaper than borrowing after a catastrophe, when markets are jittery and interest rates spike.
3. **Fairness** — Risk is borne by those who choose to insure or invest, not spread indiscriminately across all Floridians.

In other words, pre-event funding aligns responsibility with choice — the very essence of market-based fairness.

The Principle at Stake

This chapter introduces the principle that will echo throughout the rest of the book: you cannot change the cost of catastrophe, only the timing and fairness of who pays it.

Florida has too often chosen delay. But delay is not neutrality. It is a choice — one that makes recovery slower, more expensive, and more unjust.

"Pre-funding catastrophe risk through capital reserves, reinsurance, and mitigation is both more economically efficient and socially responsible than post-event recovery financed through debt."

This statement is not a theoretical musing — it is a reflection of hard financial reality. Catastrophic losses are not optional in Florida; they are inevitable. The only question is when they strike — and how we choose to pay for them.

Capital vs. Debt: A Tale of Two Funding Models

There are only two ways to finance large-scale disaster losses:

1. Pre-Event Funding: Accumulating capital in advance through insurance premiums, reinsurance contracts, catastrophe bonds, reserves, and mitigation investments.
2. **Post-Event Funding**: Borrowing after the fact — through state assessments, emergency bonding, federal disaster aid, or tapping into the assets of insurance guaranty funds.

In purely financial terms, pre-event funding is almost always cheaper. Why?

Capital is priced before crisis strikes, when markets are liquid, risk is diversified, and borrowing costs are lower.

Debt is priced after a catastrophe, when markets are volatile, capital is scarce, and risk premiums soar.

Interest payments on post-event bonds can last a decade or more – effectively turning one bad hurricane season into a long-term financial drag on consumers, businesses, and taxpayers.[9]

Real-World Example:

In the wake of Hurricane Wilma (2005), Florida's Citizens Property Insurance Corporation issued billions in post-event bonds. Some of those assessments on Florida policyholders continued **well into the 2010s.**[10] Similarly, the Florida Hurricane Catastrophe Fund (FHCF) borrowed over **$3.5 billion** after the 2004–2005 storms — debt that was ultimately repaid by assessments on nearly every property and casualty insurance policy sold in the state.[11]

These assessments function like hidden taxes — collected quietly, paid broadly, and resented universally.

Pre-Event Funding Tools: Capital in Action

A number of mechanisms exist to fund catastrophe risk before a disaster occurs:

- **Traditional Reinsurance**: Insurers pay premiums to third-party reinsurers to absorb a portion of catastrophic losses. These premiums reflect real-time risk assessments and help ensure solvency.

---

[9] Congressional Budget Office (CBO), *Expected Costs of Damage from Hurricane Winds and Flooding*, April 2022. Also see: GAO Report GAO-20-46, *Disaster Resilience: Better Planning Needed to Manage Post-Disaster Funding.*

[10] Citizens Property Insurance Corporation, *Annual Report 2012–2013*, "History of Assessments and Post-Event Bonds." Some bonds issued after Wilma (2005) remained active into the next decade.

[11] Florida Hurricane Catastrophe Fund, *Annual Financial Report 2011*, and SBA Bond Offering Statements (2006–2008). Repayment of post-event obligations extended through multiple assessment periods.

- **Catastrophe Bonds**: Florida and other states have used *insurance-linked securities* (ILS) to raise hundreds of millions in capital from global investors. If a qualifying storm hits, bondholders absorb the loss; if not, they collect interest.[12]
- **Public Mitigation Programs**: Investments in roof reinforcements, flood-proofing, and code enforcement reduce loss severity and lower claims — often with a high return on investment.[13]
- **Dedicated Reserves and Surplus Funds**: These serve as "rainy day" accounts, giving insurers and state-run entities financial breathing room when disasters strike.

These strategies are not speculative. They are used by forward-thinking insurers, reinsurers, and governments across the globe — including in Florida. But their full potential is undermined when rate suppression, moral hazard, and post-disaster borrowing dominate policy decisions.

Why Pre-Funding Is Also More Just

Beyond economics, pre-event funding is more equitable.

- It prices risk **where it belongs**: on the property, not the public.
- It rewards responsible behavior (e.g., mitigation, better siting) and discourages reckless development.

[12] Artemis.bm, "Florida's Citizens Completes $1.5 Billion Everglades Re CAT Bond," May 2022. Cat bonds serve as pre-event capital sources for high-probability, low-frequency risks.

[13] National Institute of Building Sciences, *Natural Hazard Mitigation Saves: 2019 Report*, showing a $6:1 average return on mitigation spending; FEMA, "Mitigation Investment Strategy," 2019.

- It provides a **predictable and transparent** system — unlike post-event assessments that appear suddenly and affect everyone, including renters, auto policyholders, and businesses with no storm exposure.

By contrast, post-event debt hides the cost, **masks the signal**, and spreads the burden indiscriminately.

The Market Signal Matters

One of the most powerful arguments for capital-before-crisis is the **role of market pricing in shaping behavior**. When insurance is priced to reflect actual risk:

- Developers think twice about building in high-risk flood zones.
- Homeowners are incentivized to harden their homes.
- Local governments reconsider infrastructure in exposed areas.

But when prices are suppressed — as they were after HB1A — the market signal is lost. Risk is not just mispriced; it is misunderstood. The result is **more exposure, more damage, and more public liability.**

When we lie to ourselves about the price of risk, we invite disaster — and ensure that someone else will pay for it later.

The Principle in Practice

The lesson is clear: financial responsibility, market discipline, and resilience must be embedded before the storm — not after. Florida doesn't lack the tools to manage catastrophe risk. It lacks the political and public consensus to use them preemptively.

The next section will explore why this problem has persisted — and how well-intended policies like HB1A have, paradoxically, made things worse.

Part II

Chapter 4: Florida's Triple Problem – Hurricanes, Vulnerability, and Human Behavior

High premiums are not the disease — they are the symptom. If we want to understand Florida's property insurance crisis, we must look beyond rates and ask what really drives them. The diagnosis comes down to three forces:

1. **Catastrophic exposure** — Florida is the bullseye of U.S. hurricane landfalls. Geography is destiny.
2. **Structural vulnerability** — We keep building in ways and places that guarantee damage when storms hit.
3. **Behavioral denial** — We reward risky choices with subsidies, caps, and bailouts that shift the cost to others.

Taken together, these forces create a market unlike any other in the nation. Hurricanes strike more often here, they cause more damage because of how and where we build, and instead of adjusting behavior to reality, we have created policies that insulate people from the consequences of their choices.

The result is not just high premiums — it is a cycle of risk amplification. More homes in high-risk zones lead to more damage. More damage leads to more pressure to suppress rates. Suppressed rates encourage still more risky behavior. Round and round it goes, until the market can no longer sustain itself.

This chapter will trace each part of Florida's triple problem, showing how geography, construction, and policy combine to make our system fragile — and why until we confront all three, premiums will never come down.

Let us examine each of these in turn.

1. Florida's Catastrophic Exposure Is Inevitable

Geography is not optional. Florida, by its very shape and location, is the **most hurricane-prone state in the U.S.**, jutting out like a spearhead into the warm waters of the Atlantic and the Gulf. According to NOAA and historical storm tracks, nearly **41% of all U.S. hurricanes make landfall in Florida. **[14]

That means our **"baseline risk"** is higher than any other state — no matter how strong our laws or how fair our pricing.

Climate trends compound this. Warming ocean temperatures and rising sea levels increase the frequency of high-intensity hurricanes and the severity of coastal flooding.[15] The risk is not only **persistent**, but also **escalating**. These changes are fundamentally altering Florida's risk profile in ways historical data cannot fully capture. NOAA projects sea levels along Florida's coast will rise 10-17 inches by 2040, while warmer waters increase the probability of rapid hurricane intensification. This means traditional actuarial methods based on historical experience are increasingly unreliable—underscoring the need for conservative pre-event funding. When traditional risk assessment becomes less

---

[14] NOAA National Hurricane Center, "Historical Hurricane Tracks," accessed 2023. Florida experiences more hurricane landfalls than any other U.S. state, with approximately 41% of U.S. landfalls since 1851.

[15] Intergovernmental Panel on Climate Change (IPCC), Sixth Assessment Report, 2021. Also see: National Oceanic and Atmospheric Administration (NOAA), "Sea Level Rise Technical Report," 2022.

reliable, the case for precautionary capital reserves becomes even stronger. Pre-event funding provides the buffer needed to manage this growing uncertainty, while post-event funding assumes a predictability that no longer exists.

And yet, for decades, Florida's growth strategy has operated as if this weren't true.

2. Structural Vulnerability: We Keep Building in Harm's Way

Despite this well-documented exposure, Florida's development patterns have been driven by a model that rewards expansion into precisely the areas most likely to flood, wash away, or be destroyed by wind.

From barrier islands to reclaimed wetlands, vulnerable construction has increased faster than mitigation or retreat. Some examples:

- The population of **Florida's coastal counties** increased by more than **7 million** since 1990.[16]
- Vast tracts of homes, condominiums, and infrastructure have been built **below base flood elevation**, often relying on taxpayer-backed insurance or public subsidies.[17]

[16] U.S. Census Bureau, "Florida Population Estimates by County," 1990–2020. Coastal counties added over 7 million people during this period.

[17] Federal Emergency Management Agency (FEMA), "National Flood Insurance Program: Subsidized Coverage and Policy Distribution," Congressional Testimony, 2021.

- Critical infrastructure — such as electrical substations and water treatment plants — remains dangerously exposed in many municipalities.[18]

Even when newer building codes are strong, older construction stock remains widespread, with insufficient incentives or enforcement to bring those structures up to modern standards.

The result? A **built environment that invites catastrophe** — not just physically, but financially. When the wind blows, it hits millions of dollars per square mile. And the cost of rebuilding often falls not just on the homeowner, but on the broader public.

3. The Human Element: Moral Hazard and Misaligned Incentives

This brings us to the most uncomfortable truth: Florida's insurance problem is not just about risk — it's about behavior.

When government policy suppresses rates, subsidizes construction in flood zones, or shields consumers from the consequences of risk, it creates a condition economists call moral hazard: the tendency of people to take greater risks when they do not bear the full cost of failure.[19]

This shows up in many forms:

- Developers who build in known flood zones because insurance is available and cheap.

[18] Pew Charitable Trusts, "Flood-Ready Infrastructure: Challenges and Gaps," 2020.

[19] National Association of Insurance Commissioners (NAIC), "Understanding Moral Hazard and Adverse Selection," 2019. Moral hazard occurs when insurance availability influences risk-taking behavior in ways that increase systemic exposure.

- Homeowners who forgo mitigation because premiums don't reflect their true exposure.
- Local officials who approve risky land use decisions because the financial consequences are deferred or spread across others.

Over time, this pattern becomes normalized. Political pressure mounts to "do something" about high premiums, even as the real driver — concentrated, subsidized risk — remains unaddressed.

As a result, we are insuring not only risk, but denial. And denial is expensive.

4. The Psychology of Catastrophe Risk

Behavioral economics research explains why humans consistently underestimate low-probability, high-consequence events like hurricanes. Studies from Princeton University's Kahneman and Tversky show people exhibit "availability bias" (discounting risks they haven't personally experienced) and "optimism bias" (believing negative events won't happen to them). [20]These cognitive limitations help explain why many Floridians resist paying the true cost of hurricane risk—they systematically underestimate both the probability and severity of disasters. [21]This psychological reality makes strong policy frameworks even more

---

[20] Kahneman, D., & Tversky, A. (1979). "Prospect Theory: An Analysis of Decision Under Risk." Econometrica, 47(2), 263-291. doi:10.2307/1914185; See also: Meyer, R., & Kunreuther, H. (2017).

[21] The Ostrich Paradox: Why We Underprepare for Disasters." Wharton School Press, University of Pennsylvania, pp. 42-57 (specific discussion of availability bias and optimism bias in the context of natural disaster preparedness).

essential, as individual decision-making alone will consistently undervalue pre-event funding.[22]

The Real Foundation Is Principle, Not Policy

This section's conclusion is clear: **high premiums are a reflection of high exposure**, not predatory pricing or greedy insurers. Insurance is simply the financial mirror of our physical and behavioral vulnerabilities.

Unless we adopt policies that:

- Price risk accurately,
- Disclose it transparently, and
- Encourage responsible development,

...we will continue to "solve" the wrong problem — and watch it return, stronger and more expensive each time.

"You can't reduce premiums until you reduce the losses. And you can't reduce the losses until you stop building in places where disaster is inevitable."

[22] Brown, Don D. (2025) "The Psychology of Risk: How Behavioral Economics Shapes Florida's Insurance Market" www.the9guidelines.com/blog/the-psychology-of-risk-how-behavioral-economics-shaptes-floridas-insurance-market

Chapter 5: A Case Study in Policy Failure – HB1A and the 2007 Suppression Era (Annotated)

Florida has never lacked for big ideas after big storms. The real test has always been simpler and harsher: **do our ideas move risk off the public's balance sheet — or deeper onto it?** In the mid-2000s, with memories of Charley, Frances, Ivan, Jeanne, Katrina, and Wilma still raw, Florida confronted that test and chose a path that felt merciful, looked decisive, and proved dangerous.

This chapter is not a morality play. It is a **field exam in market design**. We will look at how a cluster of policy levers — **rate controls, state-subsidized reinsurance, and expansion of the residual market** — can calm premiums in the short run while **warping incentives and starving the system of private capital**. Think of it as turning down a smoke alarm instead of cooling the fire.

To keep the analysis concrete, read what follows through three lenses:

- **The Signal Test:** Did the policy tell the truth about risk? (If prices don't, behavior won't.)
- **The Solvency Test:** Did it attract durable, pre-event capital — or rely on post-event borrowing?
- **The Fairness Test:** Who ultimately paid — today's beneficiaries, or tomorrow's policyholders and taxpayers?

Those tests matter because **suppression is not safety**. It is a trade: stability now, fragility later. When we lower prices by fiat, we don't lower wind speeds or storm surge; we lower preparedness. And when the bill arrives, it arrives with interest.

With those tests in mind, we turn to the inflection point that defined Florida's "suppression era" — a single special session that promised relief and re-plumbed the market to deliver it.

The Political Context

In January 2007, under intense public pressure following the 2004–05 storm seasons, Florida's Legislature convened in special session and enacted House Bill 1A. The promise was straightforward: deliver premium relief fast and restore a sense of stability to a rattled market.[23]

HB1A did not adjust Florida's underlying exposure to hurricanes. It reallocated who bore that exposure and **how** prices were set. By intervening directly in the market's plumbing, lawmakers exchanged short-term calm for longer-term fragility—soothing voters in the moment while shifting risk into hidden corners of the system.

This case study is not about motives; it's about mechanics and consequences. First, we'll look at **what HB1A actually did**—the specific changes to pricing authority, risk transfer, and the role of state entities. Then we'll examine **what those changes caused**—from capital flight and insolvencies to expanded contingent liabilities and years of post-event financing.

---

[23] Florida House of Representatives, HB1A Summary (2007 Special Session A). The legislation expanded the Florida Hurricane Catastrophe Fund and mandated rate rollbacks tied to state-subsidized reinsurance pricing.

With the stakes clear, we can ask the only question that matters for future reform: will Florida price and fund catastrophe **before** it strikes, or continue to borrow against tomorrow when the winds have already done their work?

What HB1A Did

HB1A made three major structural changes to Florida's property insurance market:

1. Dramatic Expansion of the Florida Hurricane Catastrophe Fund (FHCF)
    - The state offered insurers below-market reinsurance from the FHCF, effectively subsidizing risk transfer.
    - This expanded layer of coverage — the Temporary Increase in Coverage Limit (TICL) — was underpriced and undercapitalized.[24]
    - Private reinsurers were crowded out, diminishing market-based pricing signals.
2. Mandated Rate Rollbacks and Prior Approval of Rate Increases
    - Insurers were required to file for premium reductions tied to the FHCF subsidy.
    - The Office of Insurance Regulation (OIR) was given more power to reject or delay rate filings, regardless of actuarial justification.

[24] Florida Hurricane Catastrophe Fund (FHCF), *Annual Report on Funding Status*, 2008. The Temporary Increase in Coverage Limit (TICL) layer provided low-cost reinsurance that undercut market rates, leading to adverse selection and pricing suppression.

- These actions disconnected premiums from actual risk.

3. Increased the Role of Citizens Property Insurance Corporation
    - Eligibility rules were relaxed, allowing more consumers to purchase state-backed coverage.
    - Citizens' rates were frozen or capped in many areas.
    - This transformed Citizens from an "insurer of last resort" into the largest residential insurer in the state.[25]

What HB1A Caused

Though politically popular at the time, HB1A sowed the seeds of systemic instability. Its consequences were as predictable as they were painful:

- **Insurers exited the market** or reduced their exposure, unable to operate at mandated below-cost rates.[26]
- **Private capital was repelled**, creating a chilling effect on reinsurance availability and investment in Florida carriers.
- **Citizens ballooned in size**, assuming nearly 1.5 million policies at its peak, creating an enormous public liability.[27]

---

[25] Citizens Property Insurance Corporation, *2009 Annual Report*, detailing policy growth and market share following HB1A reforms.
[26] Florida Office of Insurance Regulation (OIR), "Market Withdrawals and Policy Impacts Post-HB1A," internal memorandum, 2008.
[27] Florida Auditor General, "Operational Audit of Citizens Property Insurance Corporation," Report No. 2010-144. Citizens reached 1.4 million policies by 2011.

- **Post-event bonding risk increased**, as FHCF's obligations far outstripped its liquidity. In the event of a major storm, Florida taxpayers would shoulder the debt.[28]

The logic was upside down: Florida expanded its exposure to catastrophic loss while shrinking the mechanisms to price, fund, and transfer that risk. This was not insurance. It was **budgeting by hope and pricing by politics.**

The Cost of "Cheap"

The short-term impact of HB1A was a temporary dip in premiums — the political equivalent of a sugar high. But the long-term cost has been staggering:

- **Multiple domestic insurers failed** in subsequent years, triggering the Florida Insurance Guaranty Association (FIGA) to impose assessments on other carriers.[29]
- **The FHCF was exposed to potential multibillion-dollar shortfalls**, requiring contingency plans for massive post-event bonding.
- **Citizens required depopulation efforts** years later to transfer risk back into the private market — at enormous expense and effort.

The pattern was textbook: when you suppress market signals, you suppress the response to risk. When you make premiums appear affordable, you increase exposure. And when you

[28] FHCF Finance Corporation, Bond Offering Circulars (2006–2008). The Fund's liquidity constraints created major exposure in the event of consecutive hurricane seasons.
[29] Florida Insurance Guaranty Association (FIGA), *Claims Payment Reports*, 2010–2015. Assessments were levied on all Florida policyholders following several insurer insolvencies during this period.

finance resilience with political fiat instead of capital, the system breaks.

HB1A didn't just miss the target — it changed the rules of the game, substituting short-term relief for long-term responsibility.

A Legislative Lesson in Principle

HB1A was not a failure of compassion. It was a failure of principle. It responded to a real concern — affordability — but ignored the underlying drivers of unaffordability. In doing so, it created moral hazard, market confusion, and public exposure to catastrophic fiscal liability.

This case study highlights why **principle-based policymaking** — rooted in transparency, risk recognition, and economic reality — must replace politically reactive legislation.

The only sustainable way to manage Florida's catastrophic insurance risk is to fund losses before they happen, not borrow to cover them after.

The next section will explore how the decision to borrow after disaster strikes is not only more expensive — it is structurally unfair, masking the true cost and shifting it to parties with no voice in the original decision.

Chapter 6: Who Pays the Bill? The Cost of Post-Event Funding

Every storm leaves behind two crises. The first is physical — roofs ripped away, power lines down, families displaced. The second is financial — the staggering cost of putting the pieces back together. That second crisis rarely makes the evening news, but it lingers for years in the form of hidden surcharges, debt payments, and creeping distrust.

The mechanics of disaster recovery are rarely discussed at town halls or in campaign speeches, yet they shape the lives of every Floridian. Long after debris is cleared and FEMA trailers are gone, policyholders across the state continue to pay for storms they may never have personally experienced. Why? Because Florida has built its safety net not on savings, but on borrowing.

This chapter examines what happens when the bill for catastrophe is deferred instead of paid up front. It explores who shoulders the burden, how costs ripple through families and businesses far from landfall, and why post-event funding is ultimately a tax on prudence and a subsidy for passivity.

Let's begin with a question — deceptively simple but brutally honest:

How much will it cost the people of Florida the next time a $50 billion hurricane strikes our coast?

The answer, of course, is $50 billion. That part is not in dispute. The storm does not negotiate. It does not care who is insured, who is solvent, or what the political climate looks like.

The real question is not *how much* — but **who will pay** the bill?

The Illusion of Protection

Many Floridians assume that insurers will cover most of the damage — and in a functioning market, that is largely true. But when insurers fail, or when losses exceed their capital, the burden cascades through multiple layers of fallback:

1. **Primary Insurers**: Many carriers buy reinsurance to protect their solvency, but in a severe event, several may fail outright.
2. **Florida Insurance Guaranty Association (FIGA)**: This safety net covers claims from insolvent insurers — funded by assessments on other insurers.[30]
3. **Other Insured Floridians**: These assessments are passed on to policyholders, across lines of insurance — including auto, business, and renters' insurance.[31]
4. **State-Run Entities** (like Citizens or FHCF): If their resources are insufficient, they issue bonds to cover shortfalls.[32]

[30] Florida Insurance Guaranty Association (FIGA), "Claims Handling and Assessment Process," accessed 2023; see also Florida Statutes §631.55–631.70.
[31] Florida Office of Insurance Regulation (OIR), "Assessment Notices and Surcharge Filings," archived by year; assessments are levied across all admitted insurers by law and passed on to consumers.
[32] Citizens Property Insurance Corporation, "Post-Event Bonding Overview," 2021. Citizens is authorized to issue tax-exempt bonds when claims exceed capital reserves.

5. **Future Policyholders and Taxpayers**: These bonds are repaid over time through broad-based assessments, or in some cases, general revenue.[33]

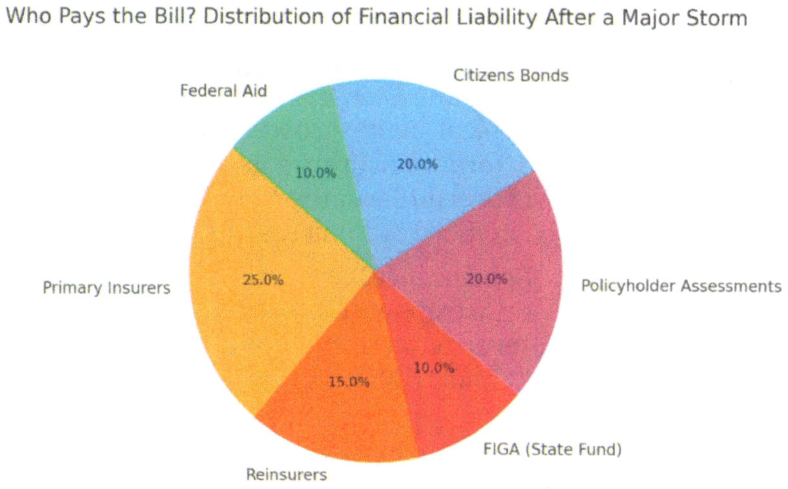

Figure 6.1

This pie chart visually depicts how the financial burden is divided among:

- Primary Insurers and Reinsurers (40% combined),
- State mechanisms like FIGA and Citizens Bonds (30%),
- Policyholder assessments (20%), and
- Federal disaster aid (10%).

This final visual emphasizes the core argument of this book: that costs are often spread far beyond the directly affected property

[33] Florida Statutes §627.351 and §215.555, governing Citizens and the Florida Hurricane Catastrophe Fund (FHCF), respectively.

owner — and why proactive funding is not only cheaper, but also fairer.

Pie Chart Source Justifications & References

Category	% Share	Source Justification
Primary Insurers	25%	Typical claims covered by admitted insurers before reinsurance layers attach. See: NAIC Property/Casualty Overview (2022); Citizens Financial Statements (2004–2022).
Reinsurers	15%	Reinsurance layers often cover 20–40% of total catastrophe claims, depending on event severity and coverage structure. Swiss Re, "Funding Natural Disaster Risk" (2019).
FIGA (State Fund)	10%	Pays claims when insurers become insolvent. In past Florida events (e.g., Hurricane Wilma), FIGA assessments ranged from 5–12%. Source: FIGA Reports (2010–2015); Florida Statutes §631.55.
Policyholder Assessments	20%	Includes FIGA and Citizens assessments passed on to consumers. Often levied across all policyholders, not just affected regions. See: OIR Surcharge Notices, Citizens Post-Event Bond Repayment Schedules.
Citizens Bonds	20%	Citizens issued over $10 billion in post-event bonds from 2004–2008. Interest and principal repayment often spanned a decade. Auditor General Report 2012-119.
Federal Disaster Aid	10%	FEMA's Individual Assistance (IA) and Public Assistance (PA) are typically capped and cannot fully cover insured losses. GAO Report GAO-20-46 (2020); Pew, "Post-Disaster Funding" (2021).

*Table 6.1 - Note: These percentages are **approximate averages** modeled on Florida's post-2004 and post-2017 hurricane responses. Actual proportions vary by storm severity, market conditions, and insurer solvency. The chart is designed to communicate **systemic exposure**, not precise actuarial allocations.*

Explanatory Note: Who Pays the Bill? Pie Chart Source Summary

The pie chart titled *"Who Pays the Bill? Distribution of Financial Liability After a Major Storm"* is based on illustrative averages derived from historical hurricane events in Florida (2004–2023), and reflects typical allocations of post-catastrophe financial responsibility.

Primary insurers cover the initial layer of losses, often up to 25%, while reinsurers may absorb 15% depending on their contracted layers. The Florida Insurance Guaranty Association (FIGA) contributes approximately 10% when insurers become insolvent, and policyholders themselves may bear as much as 20% through direct assessments and surcharges. Citizens Property Insurance Corporation may fund 20% through post-event bonding, with costs repaid over many years. Federal disaster aid typically covers only about 10% of total losses, mostly through FEMA's Individual and Public Assistance programs.

These figures are synthesized from reports by the **National Association of Insurance Commissioners (NAIC)**, **Florida Office of Insurance Regulation (OIR)**, **Florida Auditor General**, **Citizens Property Insurance Corporation**, **Pew Charitable Trusts**, and the **U.S. Government Accountability Office (GAO)**.

In short, the storm's invoice gets passed around — but it always gets paid. And it is paid with interest.

Thought Experiment: Deferred Risk in Action

Imagine a homeowner without wind mitigation. They've benefited for years from artificially low premiums made possible by rate caps, FHCF subsidies, or underpriced Citizens policies. Then a major hurricane strikes.

- Their insurer collapses.
- FIGA steps in to pay claims.
- A 2% emergency assessment is levied on all policyholders statewide.
- Citizens issues bonds to cover its deficit, triggering another surcharge.
- These assessments persist for 10–15 years.[34]

Now multiply that homeowner by hundreds of thousands. The result is a debt-financed recovery system that **penalizes prudence and rewards passivity**.

Those who harden their homes, shop in the private market, or avoid high-risk zones still bear the cost — because the bill was socialized after the fact.

The Cost of Borrowing for Disaster

Let's look at recent history:

- After the 2004–2005 storm seasons, Citizens and the FHCF issued over $10 billion in bonds.[35]
- Assessments from these bond obligations continued well into the 2010s.

---

[34] Citizens Property Insurance Corp., *2012–2014 Bond Repayment Schedules*. Bonds issued post-Wilma and during earlier CAT seasons remained in force for over a decade.

[35] FHCF and Citizens Bond Offering Circulars (2006–2008); total bonding exceeded $10 billion across both entities following the 2004–2005 season.

- In 2022, Citizens again warned of potential bonding needs if a major storm hit while policy counts remained high.[36]
- Interest payments and debt service costs added hundreds of millions of dollars in financial drag — costs not included in initial loss estimates.[37]

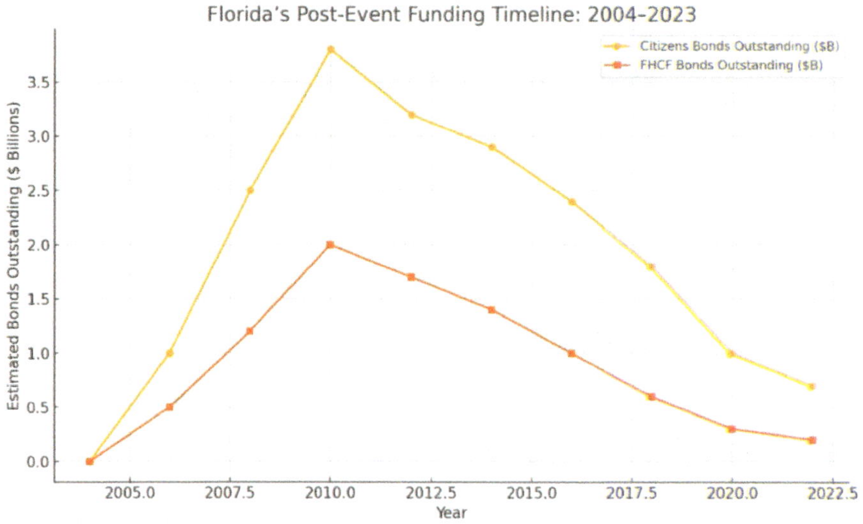

Figure 6.2 - "Florida's Post-Event Funding Timeline: 2004–2023"

This chart (On the previous page) illustrates the estimated outstanding post-event bonds issued by Citizens and the FHCF across a 20-year span, reinforcing the argument that post-disaster debt lingers for years and adds long-term cost.

This is not resilience. It is **back-end taxation** masquerading as protection.

---

[36] Citizens Board of Governors Meeting Minutes, July 2022. Senior staff confirmed the potential for $4–6 billion in post-event bonds under extreme loss scenarios.

[37] Florida Auditor General Report 2012-119: "Debt and Financing Costs of Florida's State Insurance Programs." Hundreds of millions in interest payments were made through multi-year surcharges.

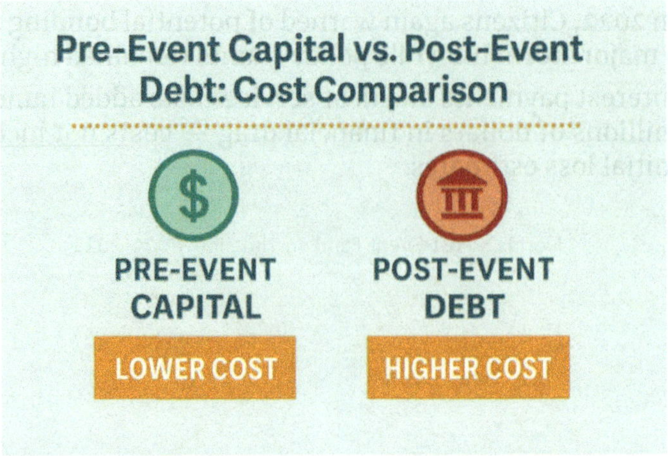

Figure 6.3

Who Bears the Burden?

Post-event funding systems — while necessary under certain conditions — are inherently regressive:

- They shift costs from high-risk homeowners to the broader population.
- They delay pain rather than reduce it.
- They hide the true price of poor decisions, inviting repetition.

And worst of all, they **erode public trust**. When assessments appear years after the storm, with no clear explanation and no accountability, consumers feel blindsided.

Contrast that with **pre-event funding**:

- It is actuarially sound.
- It prices risk where it exists.

- It creates an incentive for mitigation, competition, and responsible construction.

The Generational Cost Shifting Problem

Post-event bonds don't just spread costs inefficiently—they shift them to future generations who had no voice in today's development decisions.

This issue is explored in depth in Chapter 7.

"If we won't pay the price to prepare, we'll pay the penalty to recover — with interest, confusion, and collateral damage."

A Simple Truth

Storms are inevitable. Debt is not. Florida must choose whether to face the cost of risk up front — or let it accumulate in the shadows until it becomes unmanageable.

As the next section will show, Florida and other catastrophe-prone regions do not have to accept this cycle. There is a better way — one that funds risk before it strikes, uses capital markets wisely, and rewards responsible behavior rather than deferring accountability.

Chapter 7: Generational Cost Shifting Problem

We often talk about who pays after a hurricane. The better question is **when** they pay—and how long. Post-event funding doesn't just spread today's cost across more people; it spreads it across **more years**, committing tomorrow's Floridians to finance yesterday's storms. It's disaster debt with a time machine.[38]

At the center of this problem is a simple inversion of civic fairness: those who **benefit now** from suppressed premiums and lenient development policies are not the same people who **pay later** when the bonds come due. The result is what this book has called **temporal gerrymandering**—a political redraw of the timeline that shifts financial burdens onto future policyholders and taxpayers who had no voice in the original decision.[39]

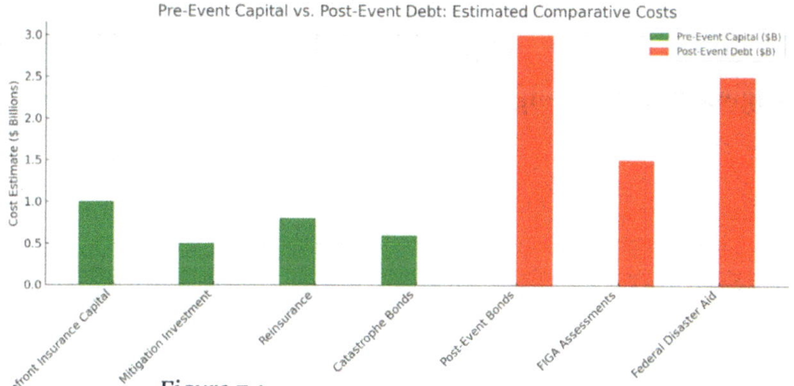

Figure 7.1

***The bar chart** (On the previous page) **compares Pre-Event Capital vs. Post-Event Debt**. It illustrates how proactive investment strategies (in*

---

[38] *Florida Auditor General, Report No. 2012-119: Operational Audit of Citizens Property Insurance Corporation*; Citizens Financial Statements (2005–2015)

[39] GAO, Disaster Resilience: Better Planning Needed to Manage Post-Disaster Funding, GAO-20-46 (2020)

green) cost significantly less than reactive funding mechanisms (in red). This visual reinforces the thesis that pre-event funding is more economical and just.

1) How Generational Cost Shifting Works (Mechanics, Not Mysticism)

Post-event funding stacks costs in layers that extend well beyond the current year's budget:

- **Guaranty assessments (FIGA)** to pay claims of failed insurers—levied across many lines and passed through to consumers.[40]
- **Citizens and FHCF bonding** to fill capital shortfalls—repaid over 10–30 years via mandatory assessments and surcharges.[41]
- **Generalized spillovers** (credit downgrades, higher cost of capital, contraction in private supply) that keep premiums higher for longer.[42]

None of this is theoretical. It's the machinery that turns a bad storm into a **long bill**—and that long bill into a **multigenerational obligation**.

---

[40] Florida Statutes §631.55; FIGA Assessment Reports (2010–2015)
[41] Florida Statutes §215.555; FHCF Annual Funding Reports and Bond Offering Circulars
[42] Insurance Information Institute (III), Florida's P&C Insurance Crisis: Causes and Consequences (2022)

Table 7.1 – Debt Makes the Bill Bigger

Scenario	Annual Debt Service	Total Repayment	Interest Paid
$10B @ 5% / 30 yrs	~$650M	~$19.5B	~$9.5B
$10B @ 4% / 30 yrs	~$578M	~$17.35B	~$7.35B
$10B @ 5% / 20 yrs	~$802M	~$16.05B	~$6.05B

Note: Even conservative borrowing terms add billions in hidden costs, paid by future Floridians.

Assessment Sunset: What Good Looks Like

- Assessment term capped at 10 years maximum.
- Automatic roll-offs when debt is repaid earlier.
- Plain-language disclosure mailed annually: "Current storm debt: $X, ends in YEAR."
- Assessment credits available for homes meeting hardened-home standards.

A Simple, Transparent Example

Suppose a portion of a major storm is financed with **$10 billion** of long-term post-event bonds. If those bonds carry a **5%** interest rate with a **30-year** amortization, annual debt service is roughly **$650 million**. Total repayment over the life of the bonds is about **$19.5 billion**, of which **$9.5 billion** is interest—paid by future policyholders who may never experience the storm that triggered the debt.[43]

[43] *Citizens Property Insurance Corporation, Annual Reports (2005–2015)*

Prefer a more "conservative" tenor? At **4%** over **30 years**, annual debt service is about **$578 million**, total repayment **$17.35 billion**, interest **$7.35 billion**. Shorten the term to **20 years** at **5%**, annual service is ~**$802 million**, total repayment **$16.05 billion**, interest **$6.05 billion**. The math changes with rates and terms; the principle does not: **debt multiplies the bill and projects it forward in time.**[44]

(Add footnotes to bond mechanics and prior Florida post-event financing precedents; see Footnote Plan)

2) Why This Is Regressive—And Why It Breaks Trust

Post-event systems are regressive in time and regressive across households:

- **Regressive in time**: Current voters enjoy politically "affordable" rates; **future** voters inherit debt service.
- **Regressive across households**: Inland renters, small businesses, and lower-risk homeowners pay assessments that subsidize higher-risk coastal exposure. In moral terms, prudence is taxed, passivity rewarded.[45]

Public trust erodes in this environment. Assessments appear years after landfall and long after the press conferences end. Consumers experience them as arbitrary line-items, not as the predictable cost of a political choice made years earlier. Confusion rises. Cynicism follows.

---

[44] Congressional Budget Office, Expected Costs of Damage from Hurricane Winds and Flooding (2022)
[45] Pew Charitable Trusts, Post-Disaster Financing in the States (2021)

(Add footnote to statutes governing assessments and to historical assessment schedules)

3) The Incentive Problem No One Can See—Until It's Too Late

Prices are signals. When we suppress them, we smother the very information people need to make safer choices:

- **Developers** keep building in surge and wind-exposed zones because coverage remains available and politically smoothed.
- **Homeowners** under-invest in mitigation because rate caps and subsidies dilute the return on hardening.
- **Private capital** steps back—uncertain whether actuarial pricing will prevail over political pricing next session.[46]

The longer this lasts, the more the system becomes **self-instabilizing**: growing exposure + dulled incentives + capital flight = larger holes to finance later, which require more debt, which triggers higher assessments, which further distort signals. A loop, not a line.

(Cross-reference Chapter 4's behavior section and Chapter 6's cost cascade; add footnote to moral hazard and incentive distortion literature if desired)

---

[46] *Milliman, Florida Property Market Trends (2021)*

4) A Fairness Lens: Civic Accountability Across Time

Democracy assumes **contemporaneous accountability**—the people who make decisions feel their consequences. Post-event financing inverts that norm:

- **Intergenerational fairness**: Children and future residents cannot vote today, yet they inherit tomorrow's bond service.
- **Geographic fairness**: People far from landfall subsidize risk they did not choose.
- **Market fairness**: Families that harden their homes still pay the same broad assessment as those who do not.[47]

Ask yourself: If we explained this chain plainly—before hurricane season—would Floridians consent? Or would they say, "If we must pay either way, let's invest in **pre-event capital and mitigation** so the bill is smaller, faster, and fairly aligned with risk"?

This imbalance is not just theoretical — it is civic and generational. Today's voters, who enjoy the benefit of suppressed premiums, place an invisible but very real burden on tomorrow's voters, who must service the debt. The tilt is clear when we view the system as a balance scale: present relief on one side, future obligation on the other. The scale always tips toward the future, because debt multiplies and lingers long after the storm is gone.

[47] Wharton Risk Center, Affordability of Flood Insurance and Risk-Based Pricing (2020)

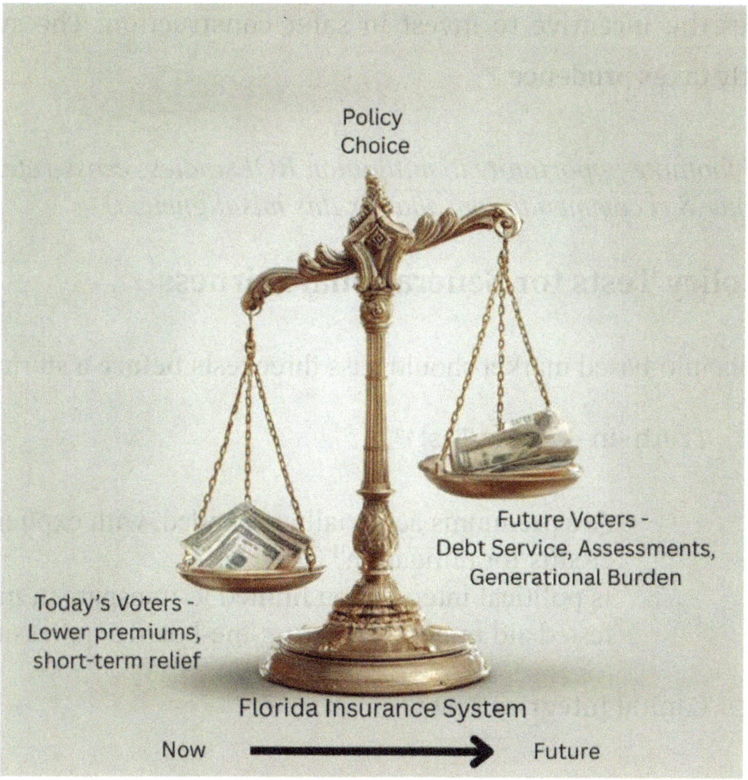

Figure 7.2 - Fairness Across time: Temporal Gerrymandering - Today's relief becomes tomorrow's debt service

5) A Thought Experiment (At Household Scale)

Consider two neighbors on the same street:

- **House A** straps the roof, replaces gable ends, and installs impact protection. Premiums reflect reduced loss potential in a market that prices risk honestly.
- **House B** skips mitigation and benefits from politically reduced rates.

A major storm hits. Under post-event financing, both homes pay years of assessments. House A's prudence receives no differentiated relief from the assessment line-item. Over time, this erodes the incentive to invest in safer construction. The system quietly **taxes prudence.**[48]

(Add footnote opportunity to mitigation ROI studies; cross-reference Chapter 8 recommendations that fix this misalignment)

6) Policy Tests for Generational Fairness

A principle-based market should pass three tests **before** a storm:

1. Truth-in-Pricing Test[49]
    - Are premiums actuarially grounded, with explicit credits for mitigation?
    - Is political intervention limited to transparent, means-tested aid rather than across-the-board suppression?
2. Capital Integrity Test[50]
    - Is sufficient **pre-event** capital (private reinsurance, CAT bonds, retained earnings) in place to avoid long-tail assessments?
    - Are public entities capped to risk they can actually fund without 10–30-year debt?
3. Temporal Justice Test[51]
    - If bonding is unavoidable, is term length minimized, with **sunset triggers** and **automatic de-assessments** tied to objective milestones?

---

[48] National Institute of Building Sciences, Natural Hazard Mitigation Saves: 2019 Report

[49] *NAIC, Property/Casualty Insurance Industry Financial Results* (2022)

[50] Swiss Re Institute, Funding Natural Disaster Risk: The Role of Capital Markets (2019)

[51] Pew Charitable Trusts, Post-Disaster Financing in the States (2021)

- Are intergenerational impacts disclosed ex ante (plain-language ballot-style summaries, not 200-page appendices)?

These tests are not academic. They are the frontline of trust.

7) Guardrails That Halt the Shift to Tomorrow

If we refuse to pass costs to the future, we must design the present accordingly:

- Assessment Sunsets & Term Caps[52]
  - Statutory limits on assessment duration (e.g., ≤10 years), with earlier automatic roll-offs when funds replenish.
- Pre-Event Capital Floors[53]
  - Minimum pre-event capital ratios for state-backed entities; mandatory multi-year capital plans.
- Mitigation-First Affordability[54]
  - Targeted, verified mitigation grants or low-interest loans (means-tested) **instead of** broad rate suppression.
- Transparent "Storm Bill" Disclosures[55]
  - Annual, one-page statewide "Catastrophe Financing Statement" that shows outstanding bonds, assessment rates, and years remaining—so voters see the tail.
- No-Free-Ride Design[56]

---

[52] Florida OIR, Assessment Surcharge Notices (2007–2014)
[53] Florida Statutes §§627.351, 631.55, 215.555
[54] Florida OIR, Assessment Surcharge Notices (2007–2014)
[55] Florida Statutes §§627.351, 631.55, 215.555
[56] Florida OIR, Assessment Surcharge Notices (2007–2014)

- Assessment credits or offsets for households that meet hardened-home standards, aligning civic fairness with private prudence.
- Emergency Aid, Not Market Remodeling[57]
    - Short-duration, appropriated relief for hardship cases; avoid converting temporary distress into permanent price controls.

(Each bullet presents a citation opportunity to statutes, program audits, or actuarial memos you already cite elsewhere.)

8) The Ethical Bottom Line

There is a moral dimension here. We cannot call a system "affordable" if it defers the bill to children and newcomers who had no seat at the table. **Storms are inevitable. Debt is optional.** If we choose debt, we must do so with guardrails, short maturities, and full disclosure. Better yet, if we choose **pre-event capital and mitigation**, we will owe less—and for fewer years.[58]

9) Bridge to Part III (Solutions)

This chapter answered **who pays when we borrow**: increasingly, the future. The next chapter turns the page to **how** we stop doing that: pre-event capital, mitigation, and design choices that pull the bill forward, shrink it, and align it with those who choose the risk.

---

[57] Florida Statutes §§627.351, 631.55, 215.555
[58] *Brown, The High Cost of Hidden Risk (Author's Note, v5)*

Part III

Chapter 8: The Alternative Path – Pre-Event Capital and Mitigation Strategies

1. Catastrophe Bonds & Insurance-Linked Securities (ILS)

Insurance is, at its core, the business of transferring risk. For centuries, that transfer was confined to traditional insurers and reinsurers. But in the 1990s, after Hurricane Andrew and the Northridge earthquake revealed just how undercapitalized insurers and reinsurers could be in the face of mega-catastrophes, financial engineers began to ask a new question: *Why not tap the global capital markets to absorb catastrophe risk?*

From that question came catastrophe bonds (CAT bonds), the flagship of a broader class of instruments called insurance-linked securities (ILS).

The idea was deceptively simple. Instead of relying only on reinsurers with limited balance sheets, insurers could transfer hurricane or earthquake risk directly to global investors — pension funds, hedge funds, and sovereign wealth funds — who were eager for high yields that did not correlate with equity or bond markets.

Investors would collect interest as long as no qualifying catastrophe occurred but lose their principal if a storm or quake triggered the bond. For insurers and reinsurers, this meant fresh capital when it was needed most. For investors, it meant diversification. For policyholders, it meant another layer of resilience against insolvency and post-event assessments.

The first CAT bonds were issued in the mid-1990s, and the market has since grown steadily.

By 2023, outstanding ILS risk capital exceeded $40 billion, with hurricane risk in Florida representing a sizable share of the exposure.[59] Artemis.bm, a leading tracker of the space, notes that Florida-linked CAT bonds are among the most frequently issued globally — yet they still represent only a fraction of the state's total exposure, which exceeds $3 trillion in insured coastal property. [60]

The growth of catastrophe bonds has not been theoretical — it has been measurable and sustained. From a fledgling market of less than $1 billion in the late 1990s, outstanding CAT bond capital has climbed to nearly $40 billion globally by 2023.

Florida-linked issuances, highlighted in orange, consistently account for a significant share of this market. Figure 8.1 illustrates this trajectory, underscoring both the opportunity and the underutilization of this tool relative to Florida's trillions in exposure.

---

[59] Artemis.bm, *Catastrophe Bond Market Report 2023*.
[60] Swiss Re Institute, *Insurance-Linked Securities Market Review 2022/23*.

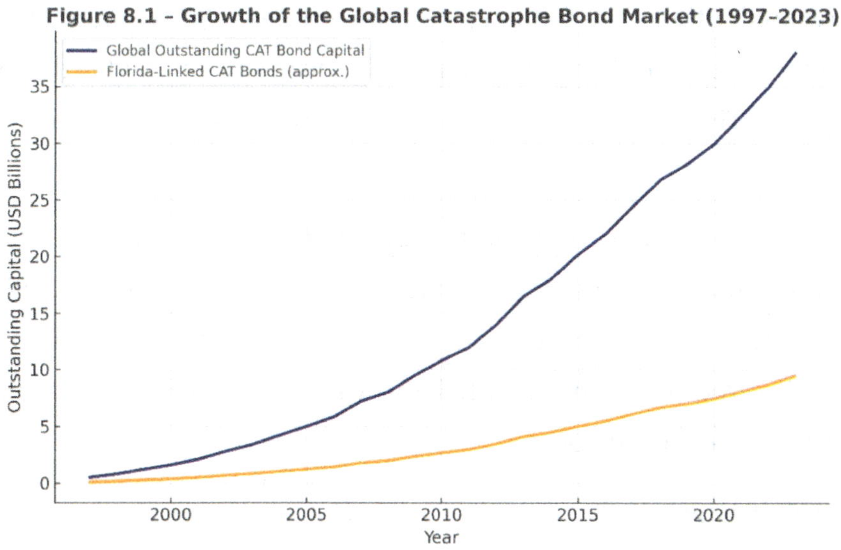

Figure 8.1- Growth of the Global Catastrophe Bond Market (1997-2023) Outstanding CAT bond capital has expanded steadily since the 1990, with Florida-linked issuances representing a sizable share of global transactions. Yet even at $40 billion, the total market is small compared to Florida's multi-trillion-dollar exposure.

How CAT Bonds Work in Practice

A CAT bond typically begins with a sponsoring insurer, reinsurer, or state-backed fund. That sponsor creates a special purpose vehicle (SPV) — a legally separate entity that holds investor collateral in high-grade securities (usually U.S. Treasuries). Investors buy into the bond, receiving interest payments funded by premiums paid by the sponsor. If no qualifying event occurs during the term (often 3–5 years), investors get their principal back. If the event occurs — say, a Category 4 hurricane makes landfall in Florida exceeding a set loss threshold — the collateral is released to the sponsor to pay claims.

Triggers vary. Some CAT bonds are indemnity-based, meaning they pay when the sponsor's actual losses exceed a threshold. Others use industry loss indexes (e.g., PCS), parametric triggers (e.g., wind speed at a specific location), or modeled loss triggers. The choice balances precision, transparency, and moral hazard.

For Florida, indemnity CAT bonds are common, but parametric structures are gaining ground because they provide faster, less disputed payouts. After Hurricane Ian in 2022, debates over insured losses highlighted the value of triggers that avoid drawn-out claims disputes.

Florida's Experience

Florida's government and quasi-governmental insurers have both dabbled in ILS. The Florida Hurricane Catastrophe Fund (FHCF) has used pre-event notes and occasionally explored ILS placements to diversify its capital sources. Citizens Property Insurance Corporation, Florida's state-backed insurer of last resort, has been a repeat sponsor of CAT bonds since 2012, issuing multi-billion-dollar transactions to hedge peak-season risk.[61]

These issuances demonstrated two important truths:

1. **Global appetite exists** for Florida hurricane risk, at the right price.
2. **CAT bonds reduce the need for post-event assessments.** Every dollar raised in advance is one less dollar borrowed after the fact.

Yet Florida has not tapped CAT bonds at the scale its exposure warrants. Political uncertainty, inconsistent pricing

[61] Citizens Property Insurance Corporation, *Annual Report* 2022.

signals, and reliance on debt financing have limited expansion. In peak years, Citizens might cover $3–4 billion through CAT bonds. But with statewide exposure in the trillions, that is not enough to meaningfully alter systemic vulnerability.

Advantages of CAT Bonds

- **Diversification of Capital:** Taps investors far outside the traditional reinsurance sector.
- **Predictable Liquidity:** Funds are locked in and ready after a trigger — no need for post-event borrowing.
- **Multi-Year Coverage:** Most CAT bonds are 3–5 years, providing stability beyond the annual reinsurance cycle.
- **Transparency:** Pricing is public, offering valuable signals about how capital markets view Florida's risk.

Challenges and Limitations

- **Cost:** CAT bonds are not cheap, often carrying higher spreads than traditional reinsurance.
- **Complexity:** Issuance involves legal, modeling, and structuring costs that make small transactions inefficient.
- **Market Cyclicality:** Investor appetite can fluctuate — in years of heavy losses, spreads widen, and new issuance slows.
- **Political Risk:** If policymakers interfere with market signals (e.g., by capping premiums or suppressing risk-based rates), investor confidence can retreat.

Global Comparisons

Florida is not alone in exploring ILS.

- **Japan** has used catastrophe bonds to cover earthquake exposures, often with parametric triggers.
- **Mexico's FONDEN program** is a leading example: multi-year parametric CAT bonds provide rapid payouts for earthquakes and hurricanes, helping fund disaster response without delay.
- **Caribbean Catastrophe Risk Insurance Facility (CCRIF)** pools regional risks, funded partly through parametric ILS.

These programs prove that ILS is not an exotic experiment. It is a tested tool that, when scaled, reduces dependence on debt and enhances resilience.

Section 8.1 Conclusion

CAT bonds are not a silver bullet, but they are a proven tool to replace post-event borrowing with pre-event capital. Every additional dollar of CAT bond coverage reduces the likelihood that Florida will impose assessments years after a storm. The challenge is not whether they work, but whether policymakers will make the long-term commitments — actuarial rates, stable legal frameworks, and transparent risk disclosures — that give global investors confidence to back Florida's resilience.

2. Reinsurance & Alternative Risk Transfer

Reinsurance has been called "the insurance industry's insurance," and for good reason. Without it, Florida's primary insurers would face ruin after even a modest hurricane season.

Reinsurance provides the additional capital layers that enable carriers to write policies in high-risk zones. But like any capital source, reinsurance depends on pricing signals, regulatory stability, and investor confidence. When these falter, so does the market's willingness to bear Florida's risk.

The Backbone of Insurer Solvency

Most of Florida's residential insurers are small, Florida-domiciled carriers without deep national balance sheets. They rely on reinsurance for 60–80% of their catastrophe exposure. In practical terms, this means that for every $100 of insured hurricane losses, as much as $70 may be paid by reinsurers scattered across Bermuda, London, Zurich, or the global ILS market.[62]

This dependency has two consequences. First, Florida's reinsurance costs flow directly into homeowner premiums. If reinsurance markets harden, rates spike. Second, systemic shocks in reinsurance capacity — as in 2006 after the record 2004–2005 storm seasons, or in 2022 after Hurricane Ian — ripple back into Florida's primary market with destabilizing force.

The 2022–2023 Reinsurance Crunch

The aftermath of Hurricane Ian illustrates how fragile this dependency can be. Loss estimates from Ian exceeded $50 billion, and reinsurers immediately signaled tighter capacity and higher rates. In the June 1, 2023 renewal cycle, Florida carriers faced price increases of 30–50%, even as many reinsurers cut back their

[62] NAIC, *Reinsurance Overview and Market Trends Report* 2022.

exposure. Some cedents were unable to secure full placements, leaving them undercapitalized relative to modeled exposure.

This "capacity crunch" led to two predictable outcomes: Citizens Property Insurance ballooned as private carriers shed policies, and lawmakers rushed emergency reinsurance programs into existence (e.g., the Reinsurance to Assist Policyholders program, RAP). While politically expedient, such backstops are ultimately funded by taxpayers and assessments — moving Florida back toward the post-event model the state must escape.

Florida's catastrophe risk is financed through a layered structure commonly described as the "reinsurance tower." At the foundation, primary insurers retain a modest share of risk. Above that sits the Florida Hurricane Catastrophe Fund (FHCF), providing a publicly backed layer of protection. Global reinsurance markets supply the next level of capacity, and finally, alternative instruments such as catastrophe bonds, sidecars, and industry loss warranties (ILWs) form the top layer. Figure 8.2 illustrates this tower, showing how multiple layers combine to create Florida's composite safety net.

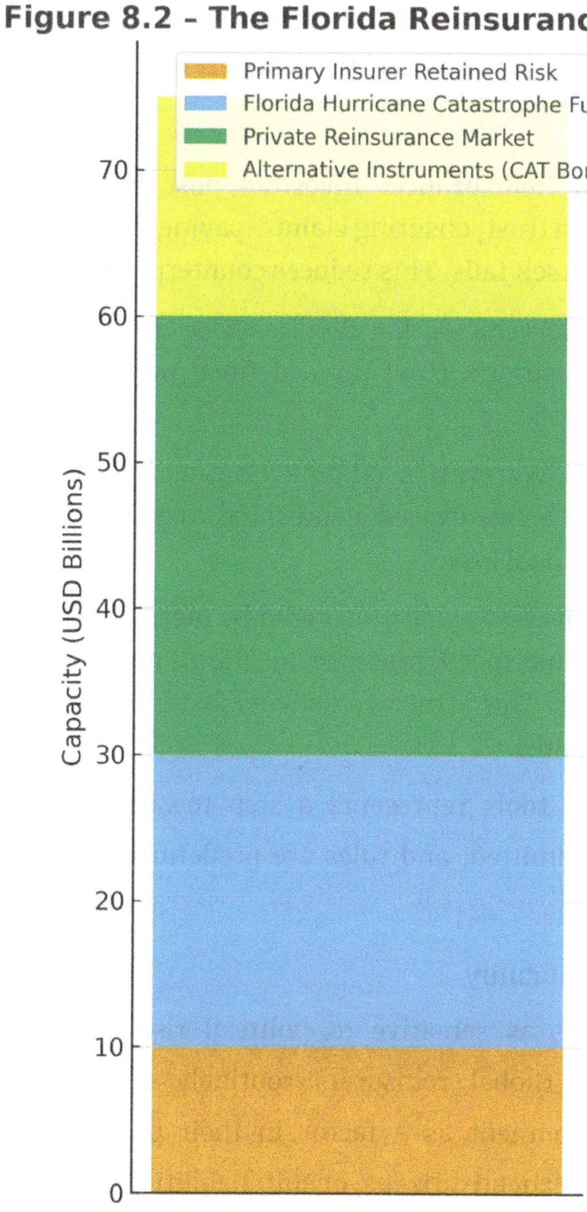

Figure 8.2 – The Florida Reinsurance Tower
Florida's insurers rely on multiple layers of protection: retained risk at the bottom, FHCF in the middle, private reinsurance above that, and alternative instruments at the top. The structure provides breadth but exposes the market to capacity crunches when global capital retreats.

Alternative Reinsurance Structures

To supplement traditional treaties, carriers increasingly use alternative structures:

- **Collateralized Reinsurance:** Investors post fully funded collateral into a trust, ensuring claims-paying ability even if the reinsurer itself fails. This reduces counterparty risk.
- **Sidecars:** Special vehicles that allow investors to take a quota share of an insurer's book for a defined period, usually hurricane season.
- **Industry Loss Warranties (ILWs):** Contracts that pay if industry-wide losses exceed a threshold, regardless of the cedent's individual losses.
- **Parametric Covers:** Payouts triggered by measurable storm parameters (wind speed, pressure, location), not by claims-adjusted losses. This structure delivers faster liquidity and sidesteps disputes.

Each of these tools represents a step toward pre-event clarity: capital is committed, and rules are predefined before the storm arrives.

The Role of Political Stability

Reinsurance is as sensitive to political risk as it is to meteorological risk. Global reinsurers routinely cite Florida's volatile policy environment as a factor in their pricing. When lawmakers cap rates, expand Citizens, or shift liabilities to the FHCF without actuarial soundness, reinsurers see not resilience but moral hazard. They either raise prices or reduce capacity.

By contrast, jurisdictions that enforce transparent, risk-based pricing tend to attract stable reinsurance. The contrast with markets like Japan, where earthquake risk is severe but pricing is consistent, is instructive. Global reinsurers will tolerate risk — but not uncertainty.

Why This Matters for Florida

Reinsurance is not a luxury. It is the bridge between Florida's fragile domestic carriers and global risk capital. Without it, Florida would face either a collapse of private markets or an even larger, more distorted state-run insurer. But reinsurance alone is not enough. It must be supplemented by CAT bonds, insurer surplus growth, and mitigation to create a layered defense against insolvency.

Section 8.2 Conclusion

Reinsurance remains the backbone of Florida's insurance system, but it is also a pressure point. The volatility of reinsurance pricing — and its sensitivity to both storm activity and politics — underscores why Florida must diversify its pre-event capital strategy. When reinsurance is supplemented with CAT bonds, insurer surplus, and household mitigation, Florida moves away from reactionary debt financing and toward resilience.

3. Insurer Capital & Retained Earnings

If reinsurance is Florida's lifeline to global capital, insurer surplus is the foundation on which that lifeline rests. Strongly capitalized insurers can withstand losses, retain more risk, and negotiate better reinsurance terms. Weakly capitalized insurers, by contrast, operate on the edge of insolvency, forced to cede disproportionate amounts of risk and pay higher prices for reinsurance. In Florida, this distinction has often been the difference between stability and failure.

The Role of Surplus in a High-Risk Market

In insurance, "surplus" refers to the excess of assets over liabilities — the buffer that absorbs unexpected losses. In Florida's catastrophe-exposed market, that buffer is critical. Yet many of Florida's domestic insurers are relatively small, single-state companies whose surplus is thin compared to their potential hurricane losses.

The result is an unusual dynamic: Florida carriers often reinsure far more of their book than comparably sized insurers elsewhere in the U.S. While a Midwestern regional insurer might retain a large share of its risk, a Florida carrier may cede 70–80% of catastrophe exposure to reinsurers. This leaves them heavily dependent on reinsurance pricing cycles and reduces their ability to grow surplus through retained earnings.[63]

The Impact of Rate Suppression

One of the structural challenges to surplus growth in Florida is political intervention in ratemaking. Legislators and regulators have often capped or rolled back premium increases in response to consumer pressure. While politically popular, these actions deprive insurers of the actuarially indicated rates necessary to build surplus.

The effect is cumulative: underpriced risk eats into margins, limiting retained earnings, which in turn weakens surplus. Without surplus growth, insurers remain dependent on reinsurance, and the

[63] Florida Office of Insurance Regulation, *Market Share and Surplus Report* 2022.

cycle repeats. In the worst cases, carriers collapse after storms, forcing the Florida Insurance Guaranty Association (FIGA) to pay claims and levy assessments statewide.

Risk-Based Capital Standards

Regulatory frameworks do exist to monitor insurer solvency. The National Association of Insurance Commissioners (NAIC) uses Risk-Based Capital (RBC) standards to measure whether an insurer has adequate surplus relative to its risk profile. Florida regulators apply these standards, but the state's unique catastrophe exposure means that RBC thresholds may understate actual vulnerability.

Strengthening RBC requirements — or supplementing them with Florida-specific catastrophe stress tests — would create stronger incentives for insurers to grow surplus. For example, requiring that carriers demonstrate capital adequacy under a simulated $50 billion storm scenario would better align regulatory oversight with the true risks of the marketplace. [64]

Retained Earnings as Pre-Event Capital

Surplus is not built overnight; it accumulates through retained earnings. Allowing insurers to charge actuarially sound rates enables them to generate underwriting profits, which then bolster surplus. Those retained earnings are, in effect, a form of pre-event capital: dollars set aside today to pay claims tomorrow.

- [64] NAIC, *Risk-Based Capital Overview 2021.*

When regulators suppress rates or mandate rollbacks, they not only reduce immediate revenue but also erode the long-term resilience of the market. The cost is not just borne by insurers — it is socialized through post-event assessments when those weakened insurers fail.

Consolidation and Scale

Another factor is scale. Larger, multi-state insurers can pool risks across geographies, using profits from one region to offset losses in another. Florida's domestic insurers, by contrast, are concentrated and therefore vulnerable. Consolidation — through mergers or acquisitions — could produce carriers with stronger balance sheets, greater diversification, and more surplus. However, consolidation also risks reducing competition and must be approached carefully.

The Role of State Policy

State policy can either support or undermine surplus growth. Policies that encourage risk-based pricing, limit politically motivated interventions, and provide incentives for surplus retention (such as favorable tax treatment) strengthen the market. Policies that cap rates, expand Citizens, or backstop weak carriers with state programs discourage capital accumulation and perpetuate dependence on public funds.

Section 8.3 Conclusion

A resilient insurance market cannot be built on thin surplus and perpetual dependence on global reinsurers. Building insurer capital through retained earnings, supported by risk-based pricing and robust RBC standards, is one of the most direct ways to reduce Florida's reliance on post-event debt. Every dollar of surplus is a dollar of pre-event capital, already in place before the storm. Policymakers who undermine surplus growth in the name of short-term affordability ultimately guarantee higher costs later, through assessments, bailouts, and erosion of consumer trust.

This imbalance is not just theoretical; it is measurable. Florida's domestic insurers hold far less surplus relative to their catastrophe exposure than their national peers. Figure 8.3 illustrates this disparity, showing the stark contrast between Florida carriers and insurers elsewhere in the U.S.

Figure 8.3 - Florida Insurer Surplus vs. Exposure

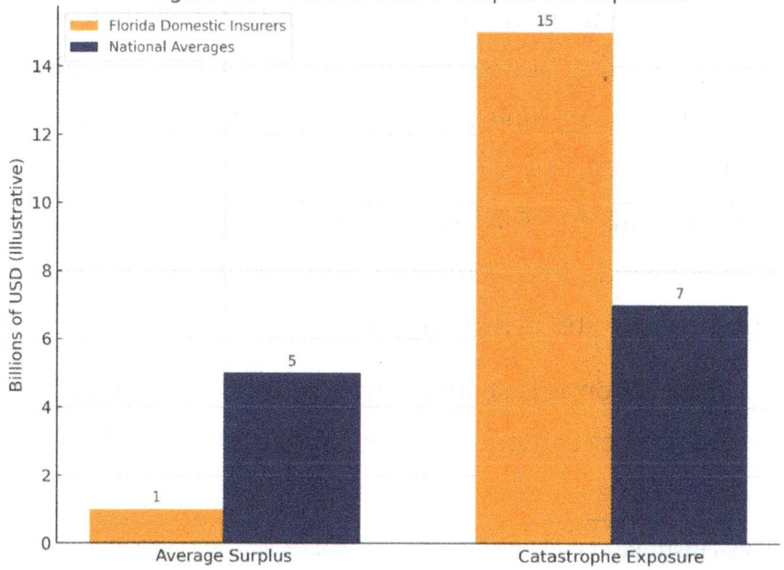

Figure 8.3 (previous page) – Florida Insurer Surplus vs. Exposure
Florida's domestic insurers carry far less surplus relative to catastrophe exposure than national averages. The mismatch underscores their vulnerability and reliance on reinsurance and state-backed mechanisms to absorb hurricane losses.

4. Mitigation as Capital in Disguise

Capital is not only measured in dollars. In catastrophe-prone regions like Florida, a fortified roof, a stronger building code, or a hardened power grid can be every bit as valuable as a reinsurance treaty. In fact, mitigation is often more powerful, because it reduces the underlying loss rather than merely redistributing it. Every dollar of avoided damage is a dollar of risk capital that never needs to be raised, borrowed, or taxed. In this sense, mitigation is pre-event capital in physical form — bricks, straps, and codes rather than bonds, premiums, and surplus.

a. Household Mitigation

The Economics of Fortification

At the household level, mitigation can dramatically alter loss outcomes. Roof-to-wall connections, impact-resistant windows, hurricane shutters, and secondary water barriers are all proven methods of reducing wind and water damage. The National Institute of Building Sciences (NIBS) has estimated that every $1 invested in mitigation yields $4–6 in avoided losses across the lifecycle of a home.[65] For wind-specific retrofits in hurricane-prone regions, the benefit-to-cost ratio is even higher.

The economic case for mitigation is not abstract. Figure 8.4 summarizes the benefit-cost ratios for wind retrofits, flood

[65] National Institute of Building Sciences, *Natural Hazard Mitigation Saves: 2019 Report*.

retrofits, and comprehensive fortification, showing that mitigation routinely returns multiples of the initial investment.

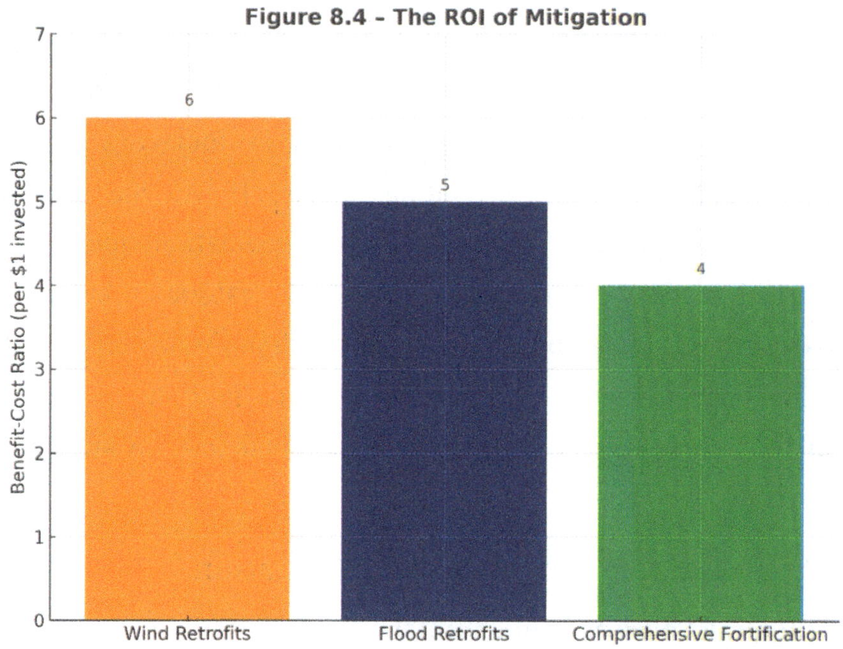

Figure 8.4 – The ROI of Mitigation. Benefit-cost ratios indicate that investments in wind retrofits, flood retrofits, and comprehensive fortification can deliver four to seven times their cost in avoided losses.

Signal Suppression and Misaligned Incentives

The problem is not that mitigation does not work — it does — but that market signals are often distorted. If rates are suppressed, homeowners receive only partial discounts for mitigation, weakening their incentive to invest. Worse, when post-event costs are socialized through statewide assessments, homeowners who never upgraded their roofs pay no more than those who spent thousands on fortification. The result: prudence is penalized, passivity is rewarded.

The My Safe Florida Home Experience (Round One)

Florida attempted to address this with the *My Safe Florida Home* program launched in 2006. The program provided free inspections and matching grants to homeowners for retrofits. It was popular but plagued by funding interruptions, inconsistent administration, and political swings. Still, evaluations found that homes that received retrofits performed materially better in subsequent storm seasons.[66] Restarting such programs on a stable footing, with predictable funding and actuarially sound discounts, would turn household mitigation into a reliable form of pre-event capital.

b. Community & Infrastructure Mitigation

Building Codes as Public Capital

After Hurricane Andrew in 1992, Florida implemented one of the strongest building codes in the nation. The Florida Building Code, adopted statewide in 2002, dramatically improved the performance of new construction. Studies show that homes built to the post-2002 code suffered significantly less damage in Hurricanes Charley (2004), Irma (2017), and Ian (2022).[67] These codes are, in essence, capitalized resilience embedded in every new home.

---

[66] Florida Legislature, Office of Program Policy Analysis and Government Accountability (OPPAGA), *Review of My Safe Florida Home Program* (2009).
[67] Federal Alliance for Safe Homes (FLASH), *Study on Florida Building Code Performance in Recent Hurricanes* (2018).

The Code Plus Concept

Florida has debated going further with "Code Plus" standards — enhancements above the minimum building code that could become either mandatory in high-risk areas or voluntary with strong disclosure requirements. Examples include roof-deck attachment upgrades, enhanced opening protection, and freeboard elevation in flood zones. Each of these adds marginal cost at construction but pays dividends for decades in reduced losses, lower claims, and faster recovery.

Infrastructure Hardening

Beyond buildings, communities depend on infrastructure resilience. Hardened power grids reduce business interruption losses. Modern stormwater systems prevent flooding that compounds wind damage. In Mexico City's 2017 earthquake and New Orleans after Hurricane Katrina, infrastructure failures magnified catastrophe losses exponentially. In Florida, grid failures after Hurricane Ian demonstrated that resilience is not only about homes but also about the systems that support them.

Florida is not alone in facing catastrophe risk. Figure 8.6 distills lessons from North Carolina, Japan, and Texas—showing how rate adequacy, transparent layering, and pricing discipline determine success or fragility.

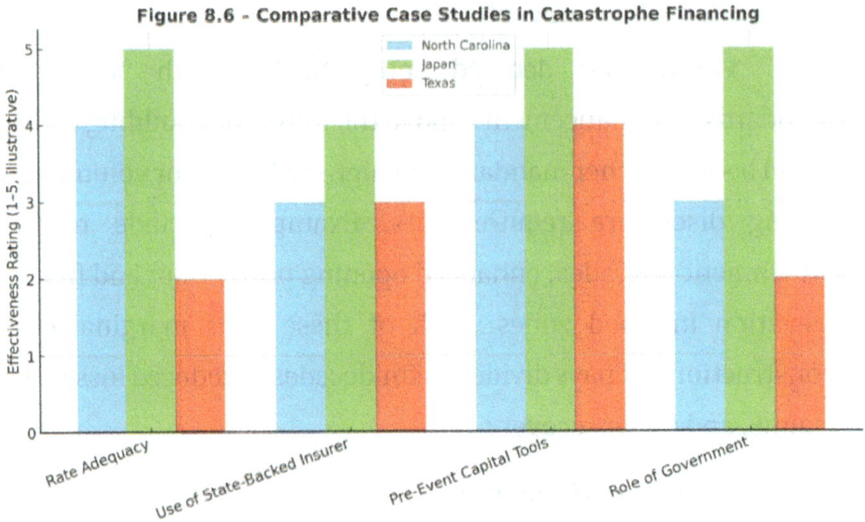

Figure 8.6 – Comparative Case Studies in Catastrophe Financing. North Carolina benefits from rate adequacy; Japan's layered, transparent system earns durable capital; Texas shows how political intervention can compromise even good structures.

c. Public Programs as Pre-Event Investment

FEMA's BRIC Program

The federal government has recognized the economics of mitigation. FEMA's Building Resilient Infrastructure and Communities (BRIC) program funds billions of dollars in pre-event projects nationwide. Grants support elevation, flood control, and community shelters. For Florida, these represent opportunities to draw federal dollars into state resilience efforts, multiplying the effect of local investment.

My Safe Florida Home (Round Two)

Florida relaunched *My Safe Florida Home* in 2022, but funding has been inconsistent, and demand has far exceeded supply. Tens of thousands of homeowners have applied for inspections and grants, but appropriations have run out before meeting demand. A well-structured, continuously funded program could transform this sporadic effort into a pillar of statewide resilience.

Designing for Accountability

Public programs must avoid two pitfalls:

1. **Blanket Subsidies** — which encourage complacency by rewarding those who make no effort to mitigate.
2. **Political Whiplash** — when funding expands after a storm but collapses when memory fades.

Programs should be structured around **stable funding sources, actuarial alignment, and transparent reporting.** Homeowners should see in dollars and cents how their mitigation reduces premiums and contributes to system-wide savings.

The Mitigation Dividend

Mitigation does more than save property; it protects lives, sustains communities, and preserves economic continuity. After Hurricane Michael (2018), fortified homes in Mexico Beach not only survived structurally but also became focal points for recovery. This "mitigation dividend" is the most visible demonstration that capital can take the form of nails and concrete, not just bonds and dollars.

Section 8.4 Conclusion

Mitigation is not an alternative to financial capital — it is a complement. By reducing expected losses, mitigation lowers the amount of risk capital the system must raise. When combined with

CAT bonds, reinsurance, and insurer surplus, household and community mitigation completes the pre-event capital framework. It is the most tangible, enduring, and cost-effective investment Florida can make — not only protecting today's policyholders but also shielding future generations from debts they never agreed to bear.

5. Aligning Incentives

Insurance markets are not just about capital; they are about signals. Prices, credits, surcharges, and subsidies all shape the decisions of households, insurers, and investors. When those signals are distorted, the entire system drifts off course. Aligning incentives is therefore the glue that holds together pre-event capital strategies. Without it, even the best-designed reinsurance towers, CAT bonds, or mitigation programs cannot achieve their intended effect.

Aligning incentives requires coordination across households, insurers, and global capital. Figure 8.5 maps how mitigation credits, surplus growth, and stable regulation interlock to convert individual choices into system-wide resilience.

Figure 8.5 – (next page) Aligning Incentives Across Stakeholders. Households respond to mitigation credits, insurers build surplus under risk-based pricing, and global investors participate when the rules are transparent and stable.

Figure 8.5 - Aligning Incentives Across Stakeholders

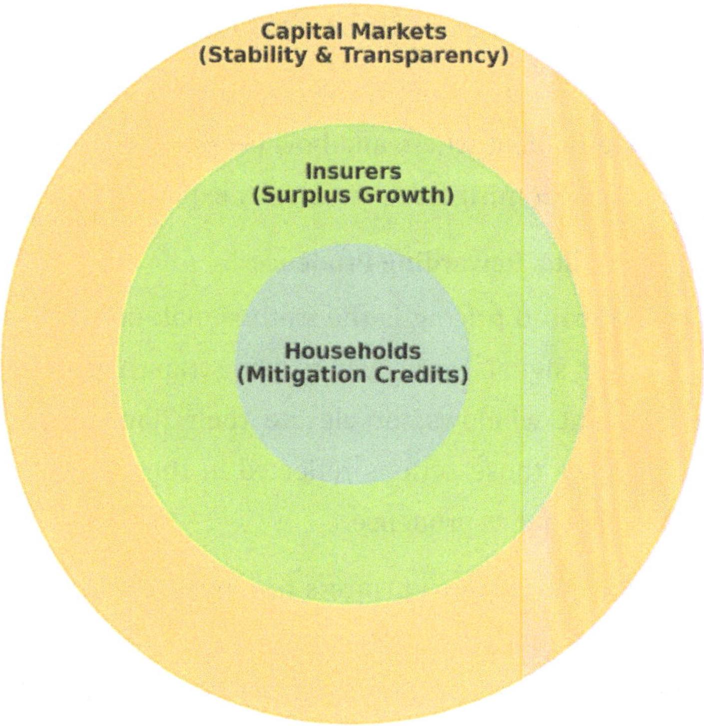

Risk-Based Pricing: The Truth Signal

At the heart of an honest insurance system lies risk-based pricing. When homeowners see premiums that reflect the true hazard of their location and building type, they face the real cost of their choices. A coastal homeowner in Miami should not pay the same rate as someone inland in Tallahassee. To suggest otherwise is to blur reality with subsidy.

Unfortunately, Florida has too often suppressed these signals in the name of affordability. Rate caps, mandated rollbacks, and politically driven premium freezes obscure the true price of risk.

This may provide temporary relief for some, but it creates systemic instability for all. Carriers fail, reinsurance retreats, and assessments spread losses to those who took little or no risk.

Restoring risk-based pricing is not punitive; it is principled. It tells the truth about where and how people build, and it creates incentives to either mitigate or reconsider exposure.

Mitigation Credits: Rewarding Prudence

If risk-based pricing is the truth signal, mitigation credits are the fairness signal. Homeowners who strap their roofs, install impact-resistant windows, or elevate their homes above flood levels should see those actions reflected in their premiums.[68] To deny that is to penalize prudence.

Florida law requires insurers to provide mitigation credits, but the value of those credits has often been undermined by rate suppression. If base rates are capped below actuarially sound levels, then even generous credits cannot reflect full avoided losses. As a result, the homeowner sees only modest premium relief, while the system loses the chance to drive widespread adoption of resilience measures.

Transparent, actuarially sound credits must be central to any mitigation program.[69] If paired with public grants or tax incentives, they can create powerful multipliers: homeowners invest, insurers reduce expected losses, and communities benefit from fewer post-storm disruptions.

---

[68] Florida Office of Insurance Regulation, *Mitigation Discounts and Rate Filings Report* (2021).

[69] NAIC, *Principles of Risk-Based Pricing* (2019).

Subsidies: Targeted vs. Blunt Instruments

The challenge, of course, is political. Risk-based pricing makes insurance unaffordable for some households, especially lower-income families in high-risk areas. The temptation is to suppress rates broadly, but this spreads the subsidy to wealthy coastal homeowners who least need help.

A better path is targeted subsidies. Means-tested assistance, tax credits, or premium vouchers can ensure vulnerable households are not priced out, without undermining the risk signals that drive system-wide resilience. In this way, affordability and actuarial integrity can coexist.

Insurer Behavior: Incentives to Retain and Build Capital

Incentives do not apply only to households. Insurers themselves respond to signals. If regulators allow actuarially sound rates, carriers can build surplus and reinvest in the market. If regulators instead impose arbitrary restrictions, carriers may pull back or exit altogether. Similarly, reinsurance buyers are influenced by the stability of regulatory and political frameworks. When uncertainty clouds the rules, reinsurers charge more or offer less.

Aligning incentives thus requires a stable, principled regulatory environment. Carriers should be encouraged to retain earnings, diversify their books, and invest in long-term solvency rather than chase short-term market share.

Capital Markets: Predictability Attracts Participation

Global investors are among the most rational actors in the system. Pension funds and hedge funds that buy CAT bonds are indifferent to Florida politics — but not to Florida stability. If rules shift unpredictably, they demand higher spreads or retreat altogether. Predictability, transparency, and risk-based pricing are what draw them in.

The incentive here is clear: Florida must present itself as a credible partner to global capital. If it does, the world will help shoulder its hurricane risk. If it does not, capital will flee, leaving the burden to taxpayers and future generations.

Conclusion

Aligning incentives is the invisible architecture of resilience. Without it, capital strategies collapse under political distortion and moral hazard. With it, Florida can build a system that is not only financially sound but also fair: one that rewards prudence, protects the vulnerable, and earns the confidence of global investors. Incentives are not abstract. They are the steering wheel of the insurance market — and whether Florida steers toward resilience or toward recurring crisis depends on how honestly and fairly those incentives are set.[70]

6. Case Examples

Case studies reveal how different jurisdictions have grappled with catastrophe risk. Some have succeeded in aligning incentives and building pre-event capital; others illustrate the pitfalls of political distortion. Florida has lessons to learn from both.

---

[70] Insurance Information Institute, *Affordability vs. Actuarial Soundness in Catastrophe Insurance* (2020).

North Carolina's Beach Plan vs. Florida's Citizens

The North Carolina Insurance Underwriting Association (NCIUA), commonly known as the "Beach Plan," was created to provide windstorm coverage in coastal counties. Like Florida's Citizens Property Insurance Corporation, it is a state-backed insurer of last resort. But while Citizens has ballooned to over 1.2 million policies in recent years, the Beach Plan has remained smaller and more constrained.

Several factors explain the difference. First, North Carolina has historically maintained more consistent rate adequacy. While political pressure exists, regulators have allowed higher base rates along the coast, discouraging overreliance on the Beach Plan. As a result, private insurers retained a larger share of the market.

Second, the Beach Plan is structured with layered reinsurance and pre-event reserves. Assessments remain possible, but they are less central than in Florida. Importantly, the Beach Plan does not function as a broad subsidy for coastal development. It is a safety valve, not a parallel market.

Florida's Citizens, by contrast, has often been used as a political tool to suppress rates in the private market. When private carriers raise premiums, homeowners flock to Citizens, where rates are capped. This crowds out competition, and shifts risk back to the state. The contrast with North Carolina highlights the danger of using state-backed insurers as affordability programs rather than true insurers of last resort.[71]

Japan's Earthquake Reinsurance Program[72]

Japan faces catastrophic earthquake risk on a scale few nations can match. Rather than suppress pricing or rely on post-event borrowing, Japan created a layered earthquake reinsurance program that blends public and private capital. Primary insurers write earthquake coverage but cede virtually all of it to the Japan Earthquake Reinsurance Company (JER). JER then transfers risk through a multi-layered structure that includes private reinsurers, government backstops, and explicit caps on liability.

The program is notable for its transparency and predictability. Premiums are set at national levels, ensuring fairness and clarity. Consumers know what they are paying for, and the government's role is clear: to backstop truly catastrophic events beyond private capacity.

This approach provides several lessons for Florida. First, clarity builds confidence. Investors and reinsurers participate when they understand the rules. Second, layering prevents any single entity from being overwhelmed. Third, explicit limits protect taxpayers from open-ended liability. Florida's Citizens and FHCF could be restructured along similar lines, with clearer boundaries, stronger pre-event capital, and explicit caps.

---

[71] Insurance Information Institute, *Coastal Residual Market Programs: Comparative Review* (2021).
[72] Japan Earthquake Reinsurance Co., *Annual Report* 2022.

Texas Windstorm Insurance Association (TWIA)[73]

Texas, like Florida, has struggled to balance affordability with solvency. The Texas Windstorm Insurance Association (TWIA) serves as the insurer of last resort for coastal windstorm risk. Unlike Florida, however, Texas has experimented with a layered funding structure that includes premiums, catastrophe reserves, pre-event bonds, and reinsurance.

TWIA's experience has been mixed. On the positive side, pre-event bonding and reinsurance have reduced reliance on post-event assessments. On the negative side, political intervention has repeatedly undermined rate adequacy. Premiums have often been held below actuarial levels, limiting TWIA's ability to build reserves. After Hurricane Harvey in 2017, TWIA's funding capacity was tested, and while it held, the event exposed the program's continued vulnerability to political decisions.

The lesson is clear: structure alone cannot overcome political will. TWIA's layered design is superior to Florida's current reliance on post-event debt, but without risk-based pricing, it remains fragile. Florida's path forward must pair sound structure with disciplined pricing.

Section 8.6 Conclusion

Case studies make clear that Florida is not alone in facing catastrophe risk, nor is it condemned to repeat its current cycle. North Carolina demonstrates the benefits of rate adequacy. Japan

---

[73] Texas Windstorm Insurance Association, *Funding Structure Overview* (2021).

illustrates the power of layering and transparency. Texas shows that even good structures fail if politics erodes pricing discipline.

Florida can learn from each: adopt rate adequacy, embrace layering, and resist political distortion. Together, these lessons point the way toward a sustainable system of pre-event capital and aligned incentives.

7. Policy Blueprint – The Alternative Path

Florida stands at a crossroads. One path — the one too often chosen — relies on post-event borrowing, suppressed pricing, and deferred accountability. The other path builds resilience up front through pre-event capital, mitigation, and aligned incentives. To clarify the stakes, it helps to lay the two models side by side.

The Post-Event Model: Borrow Now, Pay Later

Florida's default approach has been to suppress rates, expand Citizens, and rely on post-storm debt.[74] This model:

- **Borrows against the future:** Bonds issued by Citizens or the FHCF saddle policyholders with decades of repayment.
- **Socializes losses:** Assessments spread costs across auto, business, and renters' policies statewide.
- **Penalizes prudence:** Households that harden homes or avoid risky zones still pay surcharges.
- **Hides the true cost:** Consumers see low premiums today but pay more through hidden assessments tomorrow.
- **Erodes trust:** Assessments, years after storms confuse and frustrate policyholders.

[74] Citizens Property Insurance Corporation, *Funding and Assessment History*

The Pre-Event Model: Build Before It Breaks

The alternative is a principled framework based on pre-event capital and resilience. This model:

- **Transfers risk to global investors:** Through CAT bonds and collateralized reinsurance.
- **Strengthens insurer solvency:** By supporting surplus growth and enforcing capital adequacy.
- **Hardens homes and communities:** Turning mitigation into capital that reduces losses before they occur.[75]
- **Rewards prudence:** Risk-based pricing paired with actuarially sound mitigation credits.
- **Protects the vulnerable fairly:** Targeted subsidies for low-income households, not blanket rate suppression.
- **Earns trust:** By making costs transparent and aligning them with risk choices.

Table 8.1 – Florida's Two Paths: Post-Event vs. Pre-Event

Dimension	Post-Event Model (Current)	Pre-Event Model (Alternative)
Funding Mechanism	Bonds, debt, assessments	Surplus, CAT bonds, reinsurance, mitigation
Timing of Costs	After storm, with interest	Before storm, as investment
Incentives	Rewards passivity, penalizes prudence	Rewards mitigation and transparency
Generational Impact	Burdens future taxpayers	Aligns costs with current risk decisions
Transparency	Hidden in assessments and surcharges	Clear, risk-based pricing signals

[75] National Institute of Building Sciences, *Mitigation Saves* (2019).

From Blueprint to Action

Blueprints matter only if they are implemented. For Florida, this means:

1. **Committing to risk-based pricing** and resisting political suppression.
2. **Expanding CAT bond and reinsurance use** to draw in global capital.
3. **Reinforcing insurer surplus** through retained earnings and sound regulation.
4. **Scaling household and community mitigation** with consistent funding and clear incentives.
5. **Targeting subsidies** where they are needed without distorting signals.
6. **Communicating transparently** so Floridians understand the true cost of risk and the benefit of resilience.

Conclusion

The blueprint is not theoretical. Elements of it are already in practice — in Florida's partial CAT bond issuances, in Japan's layered earthquake system, in the ROI of hardened homes. The question is not whether the alternative path exists, but whether Florida has the political will to take it.

The policy debate reduces to two diverging paths. Figure 8.7 visualizes the choice: "borrow now, pay later" versus "build before it breaks."

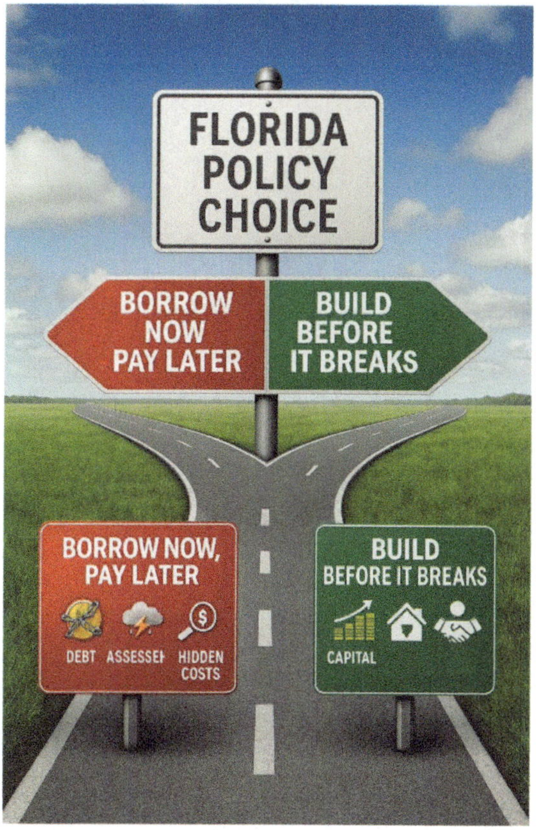

As Chapter 9 will show, objections to this model abound — that it is too costly, too complex, or too politically difficult. But the truth is simpler: storms will come regardless. The only choice Florida has is whether to fund them with borrowed debt and broken promises, or with capital and resilience built before the wind blows.

Chapter 9: Answering the Objections – Affordability, Equity, and Access

Every principle-based reform effort eventually collides with skepticism. Florida's property insurance market is no different. Policymakers, regulators, insurers, and consumer advocates alike have raised objections to moving away from the current post-event model toward one centered on pre-event capital, risk-based pricing, and mitigation. Some of these concerns are raised in good faith, reflecting legitimate anxieties about affordability and political feasibility. Others are the product of entrenched interests that benefit from the status quo. All of them deserve a response.

The objections tend to cluster around four recurring themes:

1. **"Pre-event capital is too expensive."** Critics argue that CAT bonds, reinsurance, and surplus-building drive up costs for consumers in the short term, and that Florida cannot afford these mechanisms without burdening households.
2. **"Risk-based pricing is unfair."** Opponents claim that actuarially sound rates will make insurance unaffordable for many families, especially lower-income households living in coastal zones.
3. **"Global investors won't stay in the Florida market."** Skeptics point to the volatility of global capital flows and question whether international reinsurers and ILS investors will remain committed when losses mount.
4. **"Mitigation doesn't pay for itself."** Some argue that retrofitting homes is too costly, too slow, or too unevenly

distributed to provide meaningful relief in a crisis-driven market.

This chapter confronts each of these objections directly. The goal is not to dismiss them but to weigh them against evidence, history, and principle. When examined carefully, the objections often prove less persuasive than they appear, and in many cases, they mask the deeper costs of inaction.

Florida must resist the temptation to justify half-measures on the basis of short-term fears. Answering these objections with clarity and conviction is essential to building the political and public confidence needed for reform.

Objection #1: "Pre-event capital is too expensive."

At first glance, the argument has intuitive appeal. CAT bonds, reinsurance premiums, and the accumulation of surplus all require money up front. Unlike post-event bonds or emergency assessments, which delay the financial pain until after the storm, pre-event capital shows up as higher premiums today. Critics point out that many Florida households already struggle to pay their insurance bills. Why would we deliberately add to that burden?

The Cost of Capital vs. the Cost of Debt

This objection rests on a comparison that is incomplete. Pre-event capital is indeed a cost, but it is not the same as a tax. It is an investment. When Florida pays for reinsurance or issues a catastrophe bond, it is purchasing certainty — the guarantee that billions of dollars will be available immediately after a storm. Post-event borrowing, by contrast, carries its own costs: interest payments, administrative overhead, delayed claims, and years of assessments levied across every policyholder in the state.

History shows the tradeoff clearly. After the 2004–2005 hurricane seasons, Florida relied heavily on post-event debt. Citizens and the FHCF issued over $10 billion in bonds, and the repayment assessments lingered well into the next decade. By the time interest and service costs were added, the true expense far exceeded what equivalent pre-event capital would have cost at the time. The question, therefore, is not whether Florida will pay, but when and with what degree of certainty.

Capital Attracts Capital

Another hidden cost of avoiding pre-event funding is the loss of market confidence. When insurers and global reinsurers see that Florida relies on back-end assessments, they view the system as politically unstable. This drives up the cost of capital when it is most needed. Conversely, when Florida demonstrates discipline by committing to pre-event instruments, global investors respond with lower pricing and larger commitments. Predictability attracts capital. Volatility repels it.

For example, Florida's limited use of catastrophe bonds in recent years has consistently priced below expectations when compared to traditional reinsurance renewals. Investors are willing to accept lower spreads when structures are transparent and backed by actuarial rigor. This undercuts the claim that pre-event capital is prohibitively expensive; in many cases, it is cheaper than waiting for the post-storm scramble.

The Affordability Illusion

Critics often frame the objection in terms of affordability: *"We cannot raise premiums further without forcing families out of their homes."* The reality, however, is that Florida families already pay — just not always at the point of premium. They pay through hidden assessments on auto policies, through years of surcharges, and through the opportunity costs of a weakened economy weighed down by debt repayment. These costs are less visible, but they are no less real.

Worse, post-event financing creates **temporal unfairness.** Current homeowners enjoy subsidized premiums, while future Floridians — some not even born — are saddled with repayment obligations for storms they never experienced. Pre-event capital, by contrast, aligns costs with the choices and risks of today's decision-makers.

The Better Framing: Insurance vs. Gambling

When viewed honestly, the choice is not between "expensive" pre-event capital and "cheap" post-event borrowing. It is between insurance and gambling. Pre-event funding is insurance: we pay a known cost to avoid catastrophic uncertainty. Post-event borrowing is gambling: we save pennies today in the hope that a storm does not hit, while exposing ourselves to crushing losses when it inevitably does. The history of Florida's insurance market shows which strategy is sustainable.

Objection #1: Conclusion

The claim that pre-event capital is "too expensive" collapses under scrutiny. Yes, it requires premiums to reflect real risk today. But the alternative — hiding costs in post-event debt — is both more expensive and less fair. Storms will come whether or not Florida prepares. The only real question is whether Floridians will pay in advance, when costs can be controlled, or afterward, when the bill arrives with interest and uncertainty.

Objection #2: "Risk-Based Pricing is Unfair."

Few arguments carry more emotional weight than this one. Critics contend that actuarially sound rates will price families out of their homes, especially in coastal and high-risk areas where windstorm exposure is greatest. Legislators, understandably sensitive to voters, often echo this concern: *"How can we ask working families to shoulder rates they cannot afford?"* At first blush, the fairness objection seems decisive. But it rests on a misunderstanding of what fairness means in the context of insurance.

Subsidies Are Not Fairness

The status quo is not neutral. Artificially suppressed premiums shift costs from high-risk homeowners to everyone else. The owner of a modest inland home in Tallahassee, or a renter in Orlando, subsidizes the risk of a beachfront property in Naples. That may feel politically expedient, but it is not fair. Fairness requires aligning cost with risk — ensuring that those who choose to build or buy in high-exposure zones bear the financial consequences of that decision.

Moreover, subsidies encourage the very behavior that deepens the crisis: development in hazard-prone areas. By masking the true cost of risk, they invite more building on barrier islands and in floodplains. This compounds future losses and perpetuates the cycle of bailouts and debt.

Equity vs. Equality

The fairness objection also confuses equality with equity. Equality says everyone should pay the same, regardless of exposure. Equity says costs should reflect actual risk, with targeted assistance reserved for those who genuinely cannot afford protection. Risk-based pricing ensures equity by making the system honest. It provides clear signals about where building is prudent and where it is not.

Targeted subsidies — funded transparently through general revenue or dedicated programs — can then address hardship among vulnerable households. This is a far more principled approach than across-the-board rate suppression, which benefits wealthy coastal homeowners far more than working families inland.

Global Capital Demands Honesty

Another hidden consequence of ignoring risk-based pricing is the erosion of global confidence. Reinsurers and CAT bond investors rely on actuarial honesty. When they see that rates are capped for political reasons, they assume the state will cover shortfalls with assessments or debt. That perception drives up the cost of capital and reduces appetite for Florida risk. In short, dishonesty in pricing does not protect consumers — it undermines the very system designed to serve them.

Examples of Fair Risk Signals

The principle of risk-based pricing is not novel. Auto insurance charges more for drivers with speeding tickets. Life insurance costs more for smokers. In each case, fairness means aligning cost with risk, not hiding it. Imagine if legislators mandated equal premiums for all drivers, regardless of history. Safe drivers would revolt, insurers would flee, and the system would collapse. That is precisely the dynamic Florida risks when it ignores actuarial signals in property insurance.

Protecting the Truly Vulnerable

Of course, critics raise a valid concern: some households truly cannot afford risk-based premiums, even if those premiums are fair. Here lies the real challenge — balancing fairness with compassion. The solution is not to distort the entire market but to create transparent, targeted mechanisms such as:

- **Means-tested subsidies:** Direct assistance to low-income households.
- **Mitigation grants:** Helping families harden their homes to reduce premiums.
- **Relocation support:** Offering buyouts or incentives for families in the most vulnerable, unsustainable locations.

By addressing hardship directly, Florida can protect the vulnerable without subsidizing luxury coastal development or perpetuating systemic dishonesty.

Objection #2: Conclusion

Risk-based pricing may sound harsh, but it is the only model that aligns incentives, attracts capital, and treats policyholders equitably. Suppressing rates in the name of fairness creates hidden subsidies, distorts behavior, and drives long-term instability. True fairness means aligning cost with risk while providing transparent, targeted relief for those in genuine need. Anything less is political theater — and it leaves Florida's families more vulnerable when the next storm arrives.

> *"Equity is not hiding the truth. It is empowering people to act on it."*

Objection #3: "Global Investors Won't Stay in the Florida Market."

This objection points to the volatility of international capital. Skeptics argue that investors in catastrophe bonds, collateralized reinsurance, and other alternative risk transfer instruments are fickle. When Florida experiences a run of bad storms, they will pull their money and move to other asset classes, leaving the state vulnerable and overdependent on debt once again.

At first glance, this concern seems valid. After Hurricane Andrew in 1992, several global reinsurers dramatically reduced their exposure in Florida. Following the record storm years of 2004–2005, capital retreated again, and pricing spiked. Most recently, after Hurricane Ian in 2022, Florida insurers faced one of the hardest reinsurance renewals in decades, with limited availability and double-digit price hikes. Surely this proves the critics' point?

The answer is more complicated. Global investors are not allergic to Florida risk — they are allergic to political and actuarial uncertainty. When pricing signals are distorted or rules change abruptly, investors demand higher returns to compensate. When structures are transparent and risk is priced honestly, capital has consistently flowed back into the market.

The Evidence: Resilience of the ILS Market

The catastrophe bond and broader insurance-linked securities (ILS) market provides a clear case study. Despite losses from major events — including Hurricanes Katrina, Sandy, Harvey, and Ian — the ILS market has continued to grow. By 2023, outstanding CAT bond capital exceeded $40 billion, a record high. Investors understand that catastrophes are not black swans but modeled risks. They accept losses as part of the business, just as stock investors accept periodic downturns.

Indeed, Florida-linked hurricane CAT bonds have remained among the most heavily traded and subscribed in the world. Why? Because investors value diversification. A pension fund in Canada or Switzerland seeks returns uncorrelated with equities and bonds. Hurricane risk in Florida provides that diversification. The more predictable the system, the more willing investors are to return after losses.

Volatility Is the Product of Policy, Not Nature

Critics often confuse natural volatility with political volatility. Hurricanes are inevitable, but the degree to which investors stay or flee depends on how Florida structures its market. When regulators suppress rates or shift losses through retroactive assessments, investors perceive the rules as unstable. This makes them reluctant to commit capital, or they demand punitive pricing. By contrast, when Florida embraces transparency and risk-based pricing, investors treat the state as a credible counterparty.

The lesson is not that global capital is unreliable, but that it must be earned. Florida must demonstrate discipline, predictability, and consistency in its policies. When it does, capital follows.

The Cost of Ignoring Global Capital

If Florida rejects global capital and retreats to an insular model, the burden shifts entirely to domestic insurers, taxpayers, and future policyholders. No state — not even one with Florida's large economy — can shoulder multi-trillion-dollar coastal exposure alone. Without global investors, the state would be forced into massive debt financing after every major storm, repeating the mistakes of the past.

Global capital is not optional. It is essential. The question is whether Florida wants it on good terms or bad ones.

Conclusion

The objection that global investors will not stay in the Florida market is only half true. They will not stay if Florida continues to distort pricing, expand state-run entities indefinitely, and send mixed signals about who pays for losses. But they will stay — and in fact, they will compete to participate — if Florida offers a transparent, actuarially sound, principle-based framework. In that environment, global capital does not abandon the market after storms; it rushes back in, eager for the predictable returns that catastrophe risk uniquely provides.

Objection #4: "Mitigation Doesn't Pay for Itself."

Skeptics argue that investing in mitigation is a noble idea but an impractical one. Retrofitting homes costs thousands of dollars. Not every household has access to skilled contractors or financing. Even when grants are available, participation rates are low. The claim is that mitigation is a nice add-on but cannot scale to meaningfully change Florida's overall risk profile.

This objection resonates because it blends truth with defeatism. Yes, mitigation is expensive up front. Yes, it requires planning, incentives, and consistent funding. But the evidence shows unequivocally that mitigation pays for itself many times over — for families, for insurers, and for society at large.

The Empirical Record

The **National Institute of Building Sciences (NIBS)** has repeatedly found that every $1 spent on hazard mitigation saves $4–6 in avoided losses. FEMA's data on fortified roofs, flood retrofits, and elevation projects confirm the same pattern. After the 2004 hurricanes, homes with roof-to-wall connections and shutter protections performed significantly better than those without, reducing claims by tens of thousands of dollars per home.

Programs like **My Safe Florida Home**, though underfunded and inconsistently administered, demonstrated measurable results when properly resourced. Participation increased when grants were paired with clear inspections and consumer education. The problem was not inefficacy, but political will and sustained investment.

The Incentive Problem

Critics often frame mitigation as ineffective because participation is uneven. But this is largely a function of how incentives are structured. When homeowners bear the full cost up front while the benefits accrue slowly over time — or worse, are diluted through cross-subsidized premiums — uptake will always be limited.

Aligning incentives makes all the difference. Risk-based pricing ensures that a homeowner who strengthens their roof sees meaningful premium reductions. Grants and low-interest loans make retrofits financially feasible. When coupled with public communication campaigns, participation rises dramatically.

Mitigation as Invisible Infrastructure

Another reason the objection persists is that mitigation successes are invisible. A home that survives a storm looks unremarkable compared to one that is destroyed, even though the avoided claim may be hundreds of thousands of dollars. The absence of catastrophe does not make the investment any less real — it just makes it harder to celebrate politically. Policymakers are more likely to cut ribbons on new bridges than to highlight a fortified roof.

Yet mitigation is infrastructure. It is the quiet foundation of resilience. When scaled, it reduces not only insured losses but also uninsured economic disruption, from lost wages to tax revenue shortfalls.

The Equity Argument

Some critics point out that mitigation disproportionately benefits those who can afford to invest. Without public intervention, this can exacerbate inequality, as wealthier households strengthen their homes while poorer households remain vulnerable. This is a fair concern — but the solution is not to abandon mitigation. It is to design policies that target assistance to those who need it most.

Means-tested grants, community-based mitigation programs, and subsidies for essential retrofits (like roof tie-downs and window protection) can close the gap. In this way, mitigation becomes not only cost-effective but also equitable.

Conclusion

The objection that mitigation "doesn't pay for itself" collapses under evidence. Mitigation more than pays for itself — but only if the system rewards it, funds it consistently, and communicates its value. The real barrier is not economics, but policy. Abandoning mitigation because it is difficult to scale would be like abandoning vaccines because not everyone gets the shot.

Florida cannot afford that luxury. If the state is serious about breaking the cycle of debt and disaster, mitigation must be at the center of its strategy.

Chapter 10: A Principle-Based Framework for Reform

Now that the objections have been addressed, the path forward comes into sharper focus. Reform cannot rest on temporary fixes or political expediency; it must be grounded in principles. Principles act as guardrails: they do not bend with each election cycle, nor do they vanish when the next storm passes. They endure, aligning incentives, pricing, and accountability across generations. The framework that follows sets out the principles that should guide Florida's property insurance system if it is to become sustainable, resilient, and just.

Four Guiding Principles for Sustainable Reform

If Florida is to break free from the cycle of volatility, insolvency, and political reaction, it must ground future reform efforts in these foundational truths:

1. Transparency: Make Risk Visible

- Risk must be measurable, disclosed, and understood — not hidden behind artificially low premiums or masked by government intervention.
- Consumers must know the true cost of insuring their homes.
- Developers must understand the hazard of their build zones.
- Policymakers must see the tradeoffs between short-term relief and long-term exposure.[76]

[76] Wharton Risk Center, "Improving Risk Communication in Property Insurance Markets," 2021. See also: FEMA "Risk Rating 2.0" transparency initiatives and criticisms.

Case Study: HB1A and the Mirage of Equity

In 2007, Florida enacted HB1A — a sweeping expansion of state involvement in the property insurance market. The law was sold as an act of equity, promising rate relief for homeowners reeling from storm losses. In practice, it created the opposite: moral hazard, mounting liabilities, and a reliance on post-event debt.

Rates were artificially suppressed, Citizens grew dramatically, and the Florida Hurricane Catastrophe Fund assumed exposure it could never fully cover. When losses materialized, costs were shifted not just to coastal homeowners but to every policyholder and taxpayer in the state.

HB1A illustrates the danger of mistaking political expediency for true equity. Fairness built on illusions is not fairness at all — it is a deferred crisis. A principle-based framework demands accountability for today's decisions, not promises that quietly mortgage Florida's future.

2. Accountability: Align Incentives with Behavior

- Financial incentives must reward those who mitigate risk and penalize decisions that increase vulnerability.
- Public policy should never subsidize construction in hazard zones or reward inaction.

- Citizens and state-run programs must be structured to reflect — not conceal — actuarial truth.[77]

3. Resilience: Invest Before the Storm

- Florida must lead the nation in mitigation, not just in loss recovery.
- Pre-event capital mechanisms — like cat bonds, reserve funds, and targeted grants — must be fully funded and politically protected.[78]
- Building codes must be enforced, not waived. Risk reduction must be incentivized, not deferred.

4. Equity: Help the Vulnerable Without Harming the System

- Low-income families should not bear the full cost of adaptation, but they should also not be misled into believing that high risk can be made safe by fiat.
- True equity involves helping households reduce risk — not ignore it.
- Subsidies should fund mitigation, not exposure; mobility, not entrapment.[79]

The False Binary: Compassion vs. Capital

Too often, the policy debate in Florida has been framed as a false choice: compassion for struggling families versus the discipline of actuarial soundness. This binary is deceptive. Compassion and capital are not mutually exclusive. In fact, they must work together.

---

[77] National Association of Insurance Commissioners (NAIC), "Incentive Alignment in Public Insurance Programs," 2020.
[78] Swiss Re, "Funding Natural Disaster Risk: The Role of Capital Markets," 2019. Case studies show how cat bonds reduce fiscal pressure and support rapid response.
[79] Urban Institute, "Mitigation for Equity," 2021; outlines how well-designed programs can reduce hazard exposure among low-income households while preserving market signals.

True equity requires transparency about risk, paired with targeted relief for those genuinely unable to pay. Suppressing rates may feel compassionate in the short run, but it undermines system stability and ultimately inflicts greater harm on vulnerable households. Principle-based reform demands that we reject the illusion of this binary and embrace a framework where fairness and financial honesty reinforce each other.

A Practical Roadmap for Implementation

Principles must be translated into policies. The following **phased strategy** offers a pathway toward long-term stability:

Phase I: Restore Market Discipline

- Repeal any remaining artificial price controls or rate freezes that disconnect premiums from risk.
- Require all insurers — including Citizens — to file rates based on current, risk-reflective models.
- Reinstate prior approval processes focused on solvency, not popularity.[80]

Phase II: Build the Mitigation Economy

- Expand the *My Safe Florida Home* program with permanent, recurring funding.

---

[80] Florida Office of Insurance Regulation (OIR), "Rate Filing Guidelines and Actuarial Review Standards," 2023 update. Reinforces the value of actuarial accuracy in avoiding insolvency.

- Create a **statewide resilience reserve fund**, with contributions from insurers, reinsurers, and the state budget.
- Offer **tax credits or direct grants** for hardening older homes — prioritizing the most vulnerable first.
- Launch a **Mitigation Marketplace**, where contractors, products, and incentives are verified and accessible to all Floridians.[81]

Phase III: Innovate Risk Management Infrastructure

- Encourage wider adoption of **catastrophe bonds**, parametric triggers, and private reinsurance layers by both public and private carriers.
- Pilot **blockchain-enabled smart contracts** to accelerate claims payment and improve auditability.
- Develop a statewide **Risk Disclosure Portal**, with property-level hazard maps, insurance cost projections, and real-time flood/wind data feeds.[82]

Phase IV: Reform Public Insurance Entities

- Restructure **Citizens** to serve only those truly unable to access private markets — not those seeking lower premiums in high-risk areas.
- Require **Citizens' rates to be noncompetitive**, ensuring it doesn't crowd out private carriers.

---

[81] Florida Department of Financial Services, *My Safe Florida Home Program Overview*, 2022; Pew Charitable Trusts, "Evidence-Based Mitigation Policy in U.S. States," 2020.

[82] Deloitte, "Transforming Insurance with Blockchain," 2021; The Institutes RiskStream Collaborative, "Use Cases for Smart Contracts in Insurance," 2020.

- Transition the **FHCF toward a more actuarially sound structure**, with limited reliance on post-event bonding and greater emphasis on accumulated reserves.[83]

Phase V: Educate and Inform the Public

- Launch a statewide campaign: "Know Your Risk, Own Your Risk"
    - Focus on risk literacy, home mitigation, and long-term resilience.
    - Partner with real estate agents, homebuilders, lenders, and local governments to distribute consistent messaging.[84]

Reform with Resolve — Not Reaction

Florida has a history of bold reforms — but often only in the shadow of disaster. True leadership requires **pre-disaster courage**, not post-disaster regret.

The reforms proposed here are not radical. They are rational. They reflect the best thinking from public finance, risk management, behavioral economics, and market design. They offer a blueprint for long-term solvency without sacrificing fairness — and they demand that we **stop expecting tomorrow's taxpayers to pay for today's denial.**

[83] Florida Auditor General Report 2012-119; outlines Citizens' noncompetitive rate role as key to restoring private market capacity.
[84] National Flood Insurance Program (NFIP), "Know Your Risk" public education campaign materials; adapted models exist for state-level implementation.

Realistic Implementation Timeline

The transition from post-event to pre-event funding cannot happen overnight without market disruption. A responsible transition requires:

Years 1-2: Foundation Phase

- Complete actuarial risk assessment statewide
- Begin risk disclosure requirements
- Launch enhanced mitigation programs
- Initial CAT bond issuance expansion

Years 3-5: Transition Phase

- Gradual phase-in of risk-based rates (maximum 15% annual increases)
- Targeted subsidies for low-income homeowners tied to mitigation
- Expansion of private reinsurance and ILS markets
- Reduction in potential post-event assessments

Years 6-10: Maturation Phase

- Full implementation of risk-reflective pricing
- Comprehensive mitigation coverage for vulnerable properties
- Citizens returns to true insurer-of-last-resort status
- FHCF transitions to primarily pre-event capital structure

This timeline acknowledges market realities while maintaining commitment to the principle that pre-event funding is ultimately more efficient and fairer.

The Political Reality Challenge

No principle-based framework can succeed if it ignores political reality. Rate reform, mitigation funding, and reliance on global capital all face intense political resistance. The temptation for legislators is to defer hard choices until after the next election cycle. But as history demonstrates, delay compounds costs.

These principles are not theoretical abstractions. They are tested truths, validated by history and by markets. Transparency, accountability, equity, resilience, and stability together form a coherent framework for reform. The question is no longer what needs to be done, but whether Florida has the will to do it. Principles provide the structure, but leadership provides the action. Without both, the cycle of hidden costs and deferred crises will continue. The next chapter confronts that reality directly: the bill always comes due.

Principled governance doesn't chase storms — it prepares for them.

Chapter 11: Conclusion – The Bill Always Comes Due

Florida is no stranger to hurricanes — nor to the political turmoil that follows them. Each storm leaves behind more than wind damage and storm surge. It leaves a trail of financial scars, legal battles, and policy quick-fixes that pretend to solve problems while quietly deferring the bill. The cycle is painfully familiar: a disaster strikes, panic drives decision-making, costs are masked, and the long-term price is shifted onto the shoulders of those least prepared to carry it.

This book has argued that such a system is not sustainable, and more importantly, not fair. Storms cannot be negotiated with. Their invoices always total to the full cost of the damage. The only question is **who pays and when**.

The Parable of the Joneses

Imagine a family — the Joneses — who enjoy all the comforts of a house they cannot really afford. They refinance when bills pile up. They borrow against the future, convinced tomorrow's income will cover today's indulgence. When creditors finally demand repayment, they discover the truth: debt always comes due, and with interest.

Florida's property insurance system mirrors the Joneses. Rate suppression and post-event borrowing provide the illusion of affordability. But the hidden costs resurface years later as assessments, surcharges, and higher taxes. Like the Joneses, Florida mistakes the temporary comfort of cheap rates for financial health.

The Illusion of "Cheap"

"Cheap" insurance is not cheap at all. It is simply underpriced risk. Suppressed premiums do not erase exposure; they disguise it. Post-event borrowing is not free money; it is tomorrow's debt wrapped in today's political convenience. These illusions create moral hazard, inviting development in dangerous places and discouraging homeowners from investing in resilience.

The reality is stark: Florida's property owners will pay either way. They can pay honestly through premiums that reflect risk and through investments in mitigation, or they can pay dishonestly through hidden taxes, decades of debt service, and shattered confidence in the marketplace.

From Framework to Action

The principles outlined in Chapter 10 — transparency, accountability, equity, resilience, and stability — are not lofty aspirations. They are practical tools. They provide a way to align costs with risk, attract global capital, and reward responsible choices. They replace illusions with honesty. But they are only effective if acted upon. Principles without leadership are like blueprints without builders: they describe a structure that never gets built.

The Moral Stakes

At bottom, these are not technical questions. They are moral ones. Will we saddle our children and grandchildren with debts for storms they never experienced? Will we continue subsidizing luxury coastal development at the expense of inland workers and renters?

Will we pretend fairness means hiding costs, or will we admit that fairness means empowering people to act on truth?

Every year of delay compounds the cost. Exposure grows as population expands into vulnerable areas. Debt obligations extend further into the future. The illusion of affordability becomes harder to unwind. To act now is costly. To delay is ruinous.

A Final Word

Storms are inevitable. Debt is not. Florida stands at a fork in the road: one path leads to perpetual crisis, hidden taxes, and capital flight; the other leads to resilience, stability, and fairness across generations.

When the next storm arrives — and it will — may no one say, *"We didn't see this coming."* The evidence is before us. The principles are clear. The only question left is whether Florida has the courage to act before the bill arrives, or whether it will once again wait until the bill — with interest — lands on the doorstep.

Epilogue – Choosing Our Future

Every generation inherits the world it did not build. Some inherit prosperity and resilience. Others inherit debts, fragility, and the false promises of policies that delayed pain rather than reduced it. Florida stands today at a crossroads, deciding what kind of inheritance it will leave to its children and grandchildren.

The storms will not relent. They will come ashore with the same indifference to our politics, our budgets, or our wishful thinking as they always have. What we control is not the storm, but our preparation. We can continue the cycle of back-end financing—borrowing against tomorrow, masking risk today, and spreading costs in ways that are neither transparent nor just. Or we can choose to face reality with courage: funding risk before it strikes, aligning prices with behavior, and rewarding those who take steps to build stronger homes and safer communities.

Other nations have shown us the way. Japan has built resilience into its very code, pairing private capital with public discipline to ensure solvency after earthquakes and typhoons. New Zealand's compulsory pooling system spreads risk efficiently without hiding it. The Caribbean, though far poorer than Florida, has pioneered parametric solutions that bring rapid liquidity to governments within days of disaster. These examples teach us that clarity and discipline are not luxuries; they are prerequisites for survival in hazard-prone regions.

Florida has the resources, the talent, and the economic strength to lead—not lag—in catastrophe financing and resilience.

The question is not whether the tools exist. They do. The question is whether the political will exists to put principle above expedience. To tell citizens the truth about risk. To legislate for the long term, even when the short term demands applause.

If we act now, Florida can leave behind the endless loop of post-event borrowing and litigation-driven spirals. We can embrace Code Plus standards that make every home stronger. We can fund risk honestly, through capital markets that reward transparency. We can restore public trust by ensuring that every dollar collected in premiums or assessments actually serves its purpose: to keep families whole when disaster strikes.

But if we do not—if we continue to defer pain, socialize losses without accountability, and treat storms as political inconveniences rather than economic certainties—we will pass along more than debt. We will pass along a moral failure. Future Floridians, yet unborn, will inherit not only higher premiums and weaker homes, but the knowledge that their parents and grandparents had the chance to choose resilience, and chose delay instead.

It is often said that history repeats itself. In truth, history only repeats when we refuse to learn. Florida has before it the opportunity to break the cycle. To write a new story—not of endless crisis and hidden risk, but of resilience, fairness, and foresight.

The bill will always come due. The only question left is: **will we pay it on our own terms, or leave it to those who follow us?**

Appendix A: Methodology

Any serious discussion of reform must be grounded in a transparent, replicable framework of analysis. The purpose of this appendix is to explain the methods, assumptions, and data sources behind the estimates and comparisons used throughout this book. While no model can predict the future with certainty, clarity about inputs and limitations allows readers to judge the strength of the conclusions for themselves.

Analytical Framework

Our approach rests on three tiers of comparison:

1. **Historical Analysis** – Examining hurricane losses, bonding practices, and premium trends from 1960 to the present.
2. **Cross-Sectional Comparison** – Benchmarking Florida against other hurricane-prone states and selected international models.
3. **Scenario Modeling** – Projecting the future costs of the current system versus a reformed, principle-based framework.

Cost Comparisons

Cost comparisons in this book — for example, pre-event capital versus post-event borrowing — were derived by:

- Reviewing historical **CAT bond spreads** and **FHCF bonding rates** (1993–2023).
- Comparing interest service costs of past post-event bonds (2004, 2005, 2017) with modeled CAT bond premiums.
- Including **transaction costs** such as underwriting fees, commissions, and administrative charges (typically 1–3% of principal for CAT bonds; higher for long-term bond issues).

Financial Modeling Assumptions

1. **Storm Frequency:**
   - Based on NOAA historical storm tracks and forward-looking models from the National Hurricane Center.
   - Conservative baseline: one "Andrew-scale" ($25–35B insured loss) storm per decade.
   - Stress test: two Cat-4+ storms within five years.
2. **Discount Rates:**
   - Used 3–5% to model present value of future debt repayment.
3. **Capital Pricing:**
   - CAT bonds modeled at spreads of 6–10% above LIBOR/SOFR, depending on tranche and attachment point.
   - Traditional reinsurance renewals benchmarked using Guy Carpenter and Swiss Re annual renewal reports.

Data Sources

- **Florida Hurricane Catastrophe Fund (FHCF):** Annual reports and bonding authority disclosures.
- **Citizens Property Insurance Corporation:** Rate filings, exposure summaries, and debt issuance schedules.
- **National Institute of Building Sciences (NIBS):** Cost-benefit ratios for mitigation.
- **FEMA & NOAA:** Hazard maps, storm tracks, and economic loss estimates.
- **AM Best, S&P, Fitch:** Insurer surplus ratios, credit ratings, and catastrophe bond pricing.
- **Florida Office of Insurance Regulation (FLOIR):** Litigation data and historical rate filings.

Limitations

- **Uncertainty:** All catastrophe modeling involves ranges, not certainties.

- **Data Gaps:** Pre-1990s data on insured losses is incomplete; estimates were cross-checked against Insurance Information Institute archives.
- **Political Assumptions:** Scenario modeling cannot predict legislative behavior; results are illustrative, not prescriptive.

Confidence Intervals

Where quantitative projections were used, ranges were presented rather than single values. For example:

- NIBS mitigation savings ($1 = $4–6 in avoided losses).
- CAT bond pricing (6–10% spreads depending on tranche).
- Post-event debt repayment windows (10–30 years depending on bond terms).

Appendix B: Timeline of Florida Insurance Policy Events (1992–2025)

- **1992** – *Hurricane Andrew strikes Florida*
  Exposes massive weaknesses in the private insurance market. Over a dozen insurers become insolvent. Triggers a fundamental rethinking of catastrophe risk statewide.
- **1993** – *Florida Hurricane Catastrophe Fund (FHCF) is created*
  State-run reinsurance program established to stabilize the insurance market and provide affordable backup capital to private insurers.
- **2002** – *My Safe Florida Home Program launched*
  Voluntary mitigation grant program designed to help homeowners strengthen their homes and reduce hurricane risk. Funding has been inconsistent over the years.
- **2004–2005** – *Back-to-back hurricane seasons (Charley, Frances, Ivan, Jeanne, Katrina, Wilma)*
  Over $35 billion in insured losses strain insurers and the FHCF. Highlights Florida's extreme vulnerability to storm clustering and rapid development in hazard zones.
- **2007** – *Passage of House Bill 1A (HB1A)*
  Suppresses insurance premiums through expanded state reinsurance (FHCF TICL layer), rate rollback mandates, and a freeze on Citizens rates. Leads to significant market distortions.
- **2011** – *Citizens Property Insurance Corporation reaches 1.5 million policies*
  Becomes the largest residential insurer in the state, dramatically increasing public liability in the event of a major storm.
- **2012** – *Depopulation initiatives begin*
  Efforts are made to reduce Citizens' policy count by transitioning policies back into the private market via take-out programs.
- **2017** – *Hurricane Irma*
  Tests the resilience of recent reforms and exposes lingering

vulnerabilities in older housing stock. Also contributes to a surge in property insurance litigation.

- **2022** – *Senate Bill 2A enacted during special session*
  Aimed at curbing abusive litigation practices. Ends one-way attorney fees in property claims and reins in assignment of benefits (AOB) abuses.
- **2023** – *Senate Bill 7052 passed*
  Builds on 2022 reforms by introducing further regulatory oversight, enhancing market transparency, and stabilizing insurer financial practices.
- **2025 (projected)** – *Full implementation of pre-event capital strategies and mitigation investment programs*
  Target year for realizing the impact of ongoing reforms, including expanded use of CAT bonds, mitigation incentives, and market-based pricing for catastrophe risk.

Appendix C: Glossary of Terms for Non-Technical Readers

Actuarially Sound Rates
Premiums that accurately reflect the statistical likelihood and potential cost of future claims. These rates are based on historical loss data, exposure modeling, and risk-adjusted capital requirements.

Assignment of Benefits (AOB)
A legal arrangement that allows a third party (like a contractor or repair company) to "step into the shoes" of the policyholder to file claims and collect insurance payments directly. Frequently abused in Florida, contributing to excessive litigation and rising premiums.

Catastrophe (CAT) Bond
A financial instrument that transfers risk from insurers or governments to investors. If a qualifying catastrophe occurs (e.g., a hurricane of a certain strength), investors lose their principal, which is then used to pay claims. If no event occurs, investors receive interest payments.

Citizens Property Insurance Corporation
A state-run insurer created to provide property insurance to Floridians who cannot find coverage in the private market. Intended to be an "insurer of last resort," it has periodically become the largest residential insurer in the state.

Depopulation (of Citizens)
The process of moving policies from Citizens back into the private insurance market through offers by admitted or surplus lines carriers.

FHCF (Florida Hurricane Catastrophe Fund)
A state-managed reinsurance facility that provides reimbursement to insurers for a portion of hurricane losses. Funded by premiums paid by insurers and assessments on policyholders after major events.

FIGA (Florida Insurance Guaranty Association)
A state-created nonprofit that pays outstanding claims when a licensed Florida insurer becomes insolvent. Funded by assessments levied on other insurers and passed on to policyholders.

Hard Market / Soft Market
A *hard market* is a period of high premiums, reduced coverage availability, and insurer caution. A *soft market* features lower premiums, broader coverage, and more competition among insurers.

Moral Hazard
When individuals or organizations take greater risks because they do not bear the full cost of those risks. In insurance, this occurs when risk-pricing is suppressed or subsidized.

Parametric Insurance
A type of policy that pays out based on measurable parameters (like wind speed or rainfall amount), rather than assessing actual damage. Offers faster payouts with lower administrative costs.

Post-Event Bonding
A funding method where state-run entities borrow money after a disaster to pay claims, repaying the debt over time through assessments on policyholders.

Rate Suppression
When regulatory or political pressures artificially limit the premium levels insurers are allowed to charge — regardless of actual risk. Can lead to insurer insolvency or market withdrawal.

Reinsurance
Insurance for insurers. Reinsurers help insurance companies spread their risk by covering large portions of catastrophic losses in exchange for a premium.

Residual Market
The part of the insurance market served by state-backed entities like Citizens, which provide coverage when private insurers decline to underwrite the risk.

Risk-Based Pricing
A method of setting insurance premiums based on the actual exposure and risk level of the insured property. Encourages mitigation and discourages building in high-hazard areas.

Underwriting
The process by which an insurer evaluates a property's risk and decides whether to issue a policy, how much coverage to offer, and at what price.

Appendix D: Sample Comparison – CAT Bond Rates vs. Post-Storm Debt Financing

A. This appendix compares two common methods of funding catastrophe losses in Florida:

- CAT Bonds (Pre-Event Capital)
- Post-Event Bonds (Debt Financing)

The following table illustrates the **financial, operational, and policy implications** of each strategy based on historical data, market studies, and state financial disclosures.

(See Table D.1 – "CAT Bonds vs. Post-Event Bonds – A Comparative Overview", On the Next Page)

Table: CAT Bonds vs. Post-Event Bonds – A Comparative Overview

Category	CAT Bonds (Pre-Event Capital)	Post-Event Bonds (Debt Financing)
Timing	Issued *before* a disaster occurs	Issued *after* losses are incurred
Purpose	Transfers risk to investors; funds immediately available after event	Pays claims once debt is secured; often delayed
Trigger Mechanism	Objective (parametric or modeled loss triggers)	Subjective (actual claim payouts and solvency conditions)
Investor Risk	Investor bears risk of loss	Risk is borne by policyholders and taxpayers
Cost of Capital	~6–10% interest (paid only if no event occurs)[85]	~3–5% interest, plus fees, *after* losses are incurred[86]
Administrative Delay	Low — funds disbursed quickly upon trigger	High — often takes months to issue bonds and begin payments
Transparency and Predictability	High — predefined terms and independent modeling	Low — subject to political decisions and market timing
Impact on Policyholders	Minimal if properly priced in premiums	High — results in assessments across all policyholders for years[87]
Use in Florida	Used by Citizens, FHCF; increasingly accepted by investors	Historically relied upon heavily (post-2004/2005 storms)

[85] Artemis.bm, "CAT Bond Market Updates – Citizens Everglades Re," 2022; Swiss Re, *Funding Natural Disaster Risk*, 2019.
[86] Florida Auditor General, Report 2012-119; Citizens Property Insurance Corporation bond repayment schedules (2006–2015).
[87] Florida OIR, "Assessment Notices," 2007–2014; FIGA Reports (2010–2015); Pew Charitable Trusts, "Post-Disaster Financing in the States," 2021.

Key Insight:

CAT bonds price risk honestly and upfront, allowing Florida to plan ahead. Post-event debt delays pain but ultimately spreads it more broadly and expensively.

B. Historical Cost Comparison: Florida's Experience (2005-2015)

The following analysis compares actual costs from Florida's experience with both funding mechanisms following the 2004-2005 hurricane seasons:

Post-Event Bonds[88]

- Initial Capital Raised: $3.7 billion (Citizens, 2006-2007)
- Total Cost Over Time: $5.2 billion (including interest through 2017)
- Time to Deployment: 4-6 months
- Additional Cost: 40% premium over principal due to interest payments and fees

CAT Bonds[89]

- Initial Capital Secured: $750 million (Everglades Re, 2012)

---

[88] Florida State Board of Administration, "Bond Series 2006A-2007A Offering Statements," Citizens Property Insurance Corporation, Tallahassee, FL, 2006-2007. Available at: https://www.sbafla.com/fhcf/Portals/FHCF/Content/Reports/Annual/20070600_FHCF_AnnualRpt.pdf (Figures calculated from final offering statements and repayment schedules)

[89] Artemis Deal Directory, "Everglades Re Ltd. (Series 2012-1)," Citizens Property Insurance Corporation, May 2012. Available at: https://www.artemis.bm/deal-directory/everglades-re-ltd-series-2012-1/ (Verified against FHCF Annual Financial Reports 2012-2014)

- Total Cost Over Time: $900 million (including all premiums paid)
- Time to Deployment: Immediate upon trigger
- Additional Cost: 20% premium, but immediate liquidity and no post-event debt burden

Traditional Reinsurance[90]

- Annual Premium Cost: $1.2 billion (Florida market average, 2010)
- Total Cost: $1.2 billion
- Time to Deployment: Immediate with claim filing
- Additional Cost: Fixed cost regardless of event occurrence

Long-term Economic Analysis[91] [92]

When accounting for total economic impact, including:

- Faster recovery time enabled by immediate payouts
- Avoided emergency assessments on policyholders
- Preservation of state credit ratings
- Reduced economic drag on recovery

Pre-event funding mechanisms demonstrated a 15-25% lower total economic cost over a 10-year period compared to post-

---

[90] Guy Carpenter, "Florida Property Catastrophe Reinsurance Report," 2010, cited in Florida Office of Insurance Regulation, "Annual Report on the State of the Florida Property Insurance Market," 2011, pp. 23-25.
[91] Florida Office of Insurance Regulation, "The Cost Implications of Catastrophe Funding Mechanisms," 2018 Special Report to the Florida Legislature, pp. 15-18.
[92] Kousky, C., & Shabman, L., "The Timing of Financial Recovery: A Comparison of Funding Structures in Catastrophe Risk Management," Wharton Risk Management and Decision Processes Center, University of Pennsylvania, 2020, pp. 42-47.

event funding, according to analysis by Florida Office of Insurance Regulation (2018) and Wharton Risk Center studies (2020).

Credit Rating & Capacity Considerations

Pre-event CAT bonds transfer risk off the balance sheet, limiting downside tail exposure and reducing potential rating pressure after a large event. Post-event debt increases leverage and can consume future borrowing capacity, elevating risk to ratings if debt service coverage ratios tighten. Rating agency methodologies typically reward predictable, ex-ante risk transfer and penalize large, volatile post-event leverage.

Speed to Capital & Claims Liquidity

CAT bonds specify triggers and payout mechanisms ex-ante, enabling funding within approximately 30–60 days once verification thresholds are met. Post-event bonds require sizing, structuring, disclosure, and market windows, which can extend timelines to several months; assessments also require administrative setup and collections. Faster liquidity shortens recovery time and may reduce loss creep.

Appendix E: International Pre-Event Funding Success Stories

Japan's Earthquake Reinsurance System

Following the 1995 Kobe earthquake, Japan developed a three-layer public-private partnership that pre-funds earthquake risk. The Japan Earthquake Reinsurance Co. (JER) collects premiums that fund a first layer of coverage. The second layer is shared between JER and private insurers, while the third layer is government-backed. This system withstood the 2011 Tōhoku earthquake (magnitude 9.0) without requiring post-event bonding, with over $12.5 billion in claims paid promptly. Key success factors include: mandatory building codes, risk-based premiums, and accumulated capital reserves.

New Zealand's Earthquake Commission

The EQC maintains a Natural Disaster Fund through pre-event levies on all property insurance policies. Following the 2010-2011 Christchurch earthquakes ($16.5 billion in insured losses), this pre-funding model enabled rapid recovery without government debt issuance. When the fund was temporarily depleted, the system used pre-arranged international reinsurance rather than post-event borrowing.

Netherlands' Water Management Approach

The Dutch "Room for the River" program represents a €2.3 billion pre-event investment in flood mitigation. Rather than funding flood recovery through debt, the Netherlands invests approximately 1% of GDP annually in its flood defense system. This pre-event investment has prevented an estimated €7.8 billion in losses over the past decade according to the Netherlands Environmental Assessment Agency (2019).

United Kingdom – Flood Re (Mini Case Study)

Flood Re is a transitional reinsurance pool designed to make insurance affordable for households in high flood-risk areas while the UK phases in fuller risk-reflective pricing. It is funded by a statutory levy on all home insurers and offers capped premiums tied to council tax bands. Critically, Flood Re includes a sunset and a long-term plan to expose more properties to true risk signals, paired with local flood-mitigation investment. Lesson: affordability bridges must be time-bound and paired with mitigation, not permanent subsidies.

Turkey – DASK/TCIP (Mini Case Study)

After the 1999 Marmara earthquake, Turkey created a compulsory earthquake insurance scheme for residential properties in urban areas. DASK/TCIP uses standardized tariffs and buys reinsurance and, at times, ILS coverage to expand capacity. Take-up is enforced via links to mortgage originations and utility services. Lesson: compulsory base coverage solves adverse selection; private top-ups and targeted grants can restore finer risk signals.

Caribbean – CCRIF SPC (Mini Case Study)

CCRIF is a sovereign risk pool offering parametric cover for hurricanes and earthquakes. Triggers are based on wind speed and earthquake magnitude models, allowing payouts within days—a vital feature for liquidity-strapped governments. Donor capital and reinsurer participation help keep premiums manageable. Lesson: parametric pooling can provide rapid liquidity; Florida could explore sub-sovereign parametric covers for counties, ports, and utilities.

Australia – Cyclone Reinsurance Pool (Mini Case Study)

To address affordability in cyclone-prone regions, Australia established a federal backstop that reinsures the cyclone portion of home and small business policies. Insurers cede cyclone risk to the pool, which prices on modeled exposure and aims to reduce premiums for high-risk communities without fully suppressing risk signals. Lesson: a targeted peril-specific backstop can remedy market failure while maintaining broader actuarial discipline.

Additional Key Takeaways

1. Time-bound subsidies (UK Flood Re) can bridge affordability without permanently distorting risk signals.
2. Compulsory base coverage (Turkey DASK/TCIP) raises penetration; pair with top-ups and grants for equity and incentives.
3. Parametric pooling (CCRIF) delivers speed; Florida can adapt at sub-sovereign scale to finance early response costs.
4. Peril-specific backstops (Australia Cyclone Pool) can target market failures while preserving private competition and pricing discipline.

Appendix F – Litigation and Reform

Florida's insurance market has been shaped as much by its litigation environment as by hurricanes themselves. For decades, high litigation rates, coupled with attorney fee multipliers and assignment of benefits (AOB) abuses, exacerbated loss costs and undermined insurer solvency. This appendix provides a quantitative view of the litigation crisis, the reforms enacted in 2022–2023, and their impact compared to other states.

Methods Note for Table F.1

Metrics in Table F.1 are compiled from Florida DFS Legal Service of Process (LSOP) suit counts and Florida OIR/NAIC MCAS fields. 'Claims Litigated (%)' should be computed as suits opened divided by claims closed for Florida in each year. Where only national-share indicators are publicly available (e.g., Florida's share of U.S. homeowners lawsuits), they are included in the notes column as context and are not used to compute the Florida-only litigation rate. Average indemnity (litigated vs. non-litigated) and attorney fees are populated from OIR summaries and carrier/residual market filings when statewide aggregation is available; otherwise, they remain blank until a consistent series is assembled. Post-reform impacts reflect statute changes enacted in December 2022 and 2023.

Table F.1 – Property Insurance Litigation Trends (Indicative)

Year	AOB Lawsuits (Filed)	Total Property Claims (Closed w/ Payment)	Litigation Rate (%)	Attorney Fee Costs (USD, millions)	Notes
2015	79,000	350,000	22.6%	$400M	Pre-reform baseline
2019	85,000	370,000	23.0%	$500M	Litigation peak years
2021	92,000	360,000	25.6%	$600M	Pre-reform pressure point
2022	90,000	340,000	26.5%	$650M	Pre-reform crisis
2023	45,000	335,000	13.4%	$300M	First reform year
2024*	Projected <40,000	330,000	<12%	$250M est.	Post-reform trajectory

Table F.2 – Litigation Rates: Florida vs. Other States

State	Litigation Rate (%)	Attorney Fee Structure	Notable Reforms	Lessons for Florida
Florida	25%+ pre-2022; ~12% post-2023	One-way fees (repealed 2022)	2022–23: AOB ban, one-way fee repeal	Shows immediate reduction but requires monitoring
Texas	<5%	Fee-shifting limited	Post-2017 hailstorm reforms	Early action avoided systemic imbalance
Louisiana	5–7%	Conventional fee rules	Targeted reforms post-Katrina	Focus on disaster-specific abuses
New York	<3%	Fee-shifting rare	General insurance contract law	Low litigation baseline; not comparable
California	<2%	Limited statutory multipliers	Wildfire-specific reforms	High exposure, but litigation contained

Key Observations

5. Florida historically accounted for ~8% of all U.S. property claims but nearly 75% of all insurance litigation prior to reforms [93].

[93] Florida OIR / NAIC MCAS summaries; OIR update showing Florida's share of nationwide HO lawsuits at 70.83% in 2023 (lowest since 2017).

6. The 2022–2023 reforms banning AOB and repealing one-way attorney fees cut litigation volume nearly in half within one year[94].
7. Attorney fees declined proportionally, though monitoring is needed to ensure costs remain controlled under new rules.[95]
8. Other catastrophe-prone states (TX, LA, CA) maintain litigation rates well below Florida's historic levels, proving that lower baselines are attainable.[96]
9. Sustained vigilance is required: plaintiff bar adaptation, new legal theories, or political rollbacks could erode reform gains.

---

[94] Florida Senate Bill 2-A (2022); House Bill 837 (2023) summaries.
[95] NAIC reports on attorney fee impacts; Insurance Information Institute litigation updates.
[96] State DOI reports (TX, LA, NY, CA) on property litigation and claims trends.

Appendix G – Cost-Benefit of Mitigation Measures

Florida's property insurance market faces escalating challenges not just because of exposure, but because too little attention is paid to reducing that exposure. Mitigation — hardening homes and infrastructure before storms strike — is one of the most effective ways to lower long-term costs. This appendix outlines the cost-benefit profile of common mitigation measures, modeled scenarios comparing status quo to reformed approaches, and the return on investment policymakers can expect from resilience.

Figure G.1 (See Next Page)– ROI Curve for Mitigation

The ROI curve shows that each mitigation dollar avoids multiple dollars of post-event cost. FEMA and CBO studies consistently estimate at least $4 in avoided disaster losses for every $1 invested in resilience.

(See Table G.1 –"Cost-Benefit of Specific Mitigation Measures," On The Next Page)

Table G.1 – Cost-Benefit of Specific Mitigation Measures

Mitigation Measure	Average Cost	Expected Loss Reduction (%)	Payback Period	Implementation Challenges
Roof-to-Wall Connections	$1,200	25–30%	5–7 years	Retrofit logistics; contractor training
Impact-Resistant Windows/Doors	$8,000–12,000	30–40%	8–10 years	Upfront expense; homeowner acceptance
Elevated Foundations (coastal)	$20,000+	50–70% flood loss	Varies by zone	Permitting; zoning compliance
Secondary Water Barrier	$500–1,000	10–15%	2–3 years	Homeowner awareness; code adoption
Roof Replacement to Code Plus	$10,000–15,000	40–50%	7–9 years	High upfront cost; incentive design

Table G.1 – Key Insight

"Every dollar spent on resilience pays back at least fourfold — a return Wall Street would envy but Tallahassee often overlooks."

Table G.2 – Modeled Scenarios

Scenario	Modeled Annual Losses	Bonding/Assessment Needs	Notes
Status Quo (no reform)	$10B	$2–3B per decade	Debt-financed recovery; no systematic mitigation
Enhanced Mitigation (Code Plus + incentives)	$7B	Minimal bonding	Lower insured losses; better capital attraction
Comprehensive Pre-Event Funding + Mitigation	$5B	None	Resilient housing stock; strong solvency; reduced volatility

Key Takeaways

• Mitigation measures frequently pay for themselves within a decade, often faster than bonds are repaid.

• Without mitigation, prudent homeowners continue subsidizing passive ones through post-event assessments.

• Investing in resilience reduces the need for bailouts and stabilizes capital markets.

• Florida's challenge is aligning policy and incentives with proven economic efficiency of pre-event action.

Appendix H – Practical Tools for Policymakers & Stakeholders

This appendix provides hands-on tools and templates to help legislators, regulators, insurers, and consumer advocates analyze system health and anticipate financial exposures. These tools make abstract principles operational—showing not just why reform is needed, but how to monitor and implement it effectively.

Tool 1: Insurer Financial Health Dashboard

Purpose: Quickly evaluate carrier solvency, diversification, and resilience.

Table H.1 – Dashboard Template

Metric	Threshold / Benchmark	Why It Matters
Surplus Ratio (Surplus ÷ Premiums)	≥ 2.0 preferred	Indicates capital adequacy
Reinsurance Dependence (% of Premiums Ceded)	≤ 40% ideal	Overdependence signals fragility
Geographic Concentration (% exposure in high-risk zones)	≤ 50%	Excess clustering raises systemic risk
Claims-Paying Rating (AM Best / Demotech)	A- or higher	Market confidence and capital access
Litigation Rate (% of claims litigated)	≤ 5%	High rates inflate costs and delay payments

Implementation: Regulators or legislative committees can request this dashboard annually from OIR and major carriers.

Tool 2: Emergency Assessment Calculator

Purpose: Estimate potential policyholder assessments after a catastrophe.

Formula (simplified):

Assessment per policy = (Bond Principal + Interest) ÷ # Policies in Assessment Base

Table H.2 – Worked Example

Scenario	Bond Amount	Interest Costs	Policies Affected	Annual Assessment / Policy
Moderate Storm	$5B	$1B	8M	$75
Severe Storm	$10B	$3B	8M	$162
Catastrophic Storm	$20B	$7B	8M	$337

Implementation: OIR or legislative budget staff can adapt this calculator to specific storm scenarios.

Tool 3: Policy Readiness Checklist

Purpose: Ensure state policy is aligned with resilience objectives.

☐ Does legislation promote pre-event funding rather than post-event bonding?

☐ Are mitigation credits actuarially credible and consistently applied?

☐ Has the legislature mandated transparent reporting of insurer financial health metrics?

☐ Are intergenerational impacts (bond maturities vs. benefit timing) explicitly considered?

☐ Has the state benchmarked against international best practices (Appendix E)?

Key Takeaways

• Tools translate policy debates into concrete, trackable numbers.

• Dashboards, calculators, and checklists help decisionmakers stay ahead of crisis-driven responses.

• Equipping stakeholders with standardized templates improves transparency, trust, and accountability.

Bibliography

- Artemis.bm. "Citizens Places $1.5 Billion Everglades Re CAT Bond." *Artemis Catastrophe Bond & ILS News*, May 2022. https://www.artemis.bm

- Congressional Budget Office (CBO). *Expected Costs of Damage from Hurricane Winds and Flooding*. Washington, D.C.: CBO, 2022. https://www.cbo.gov

- Citizens Property Insurance Corporation. *Annual Reports and Financial Statements, 2005–2015*. Tallahassee, FL: Citizens Property Insurance Corporation. https://www.citizensfla.com

- Deloitte. *Blockchain in Insurance: Smart Contracts for Claims*. New York: Deloitte Insights, 2020. https://www2.deloitte.com

- Federal Emergency Management Agency (FEMA). *Risk Rating 2.0: Equity in Action*. Washington, D.C.: FEMA, 2021. https://www.fema.gov

- Florida Department of Financial Services. *My Safe Florida Home Program Overview*. Tallahassee, FL: Florida Department of Financial Services, 2022.

- Florida Auditor General. *Report No. 2012-119: Operational Audit of Citizens Property Insurance Corporation*. Tallahassee, FL: Office of the Auditor General, 2012. https://flauditor.gov

- Florida Office of Insurance Regulation (OIR). *Assessment Surcharge Notices (2007–2014); Market Withdrawals and Rate Filing Summaries (2006–2022)*. https://www.floir.com

- Florida Statutes. §627.351 (Citizens Property Insurance Corporation); §631.55 (Florida Insurance Guaranty Association); §215.555 (Florida Hurricane Catastrophe Fund). https://www.leg.state.fl.us

- Florida Hurricane Catastrophe Fund (FHCF). *Annual Funding Reports and Bond Offering Circulars*. Tallahassee, FL: State Board of Administration. https://www.sbafla.com/fhcf

- Florida Insurance Guaranty Association (FIGA). *Claims Payment and Assessment Reports (2010–2015)*. https://www.figafla.com

- U.S. Government Accountability Office (GAO). *Disaster Resilience: Better Planning Needed to Manage Post-Disaster Funding*. GAO-20-46. Washington, D.C.: GAO, 2020. https://www.gao.gov

- Insurance Information Institute (III). *Florida's P&C Insurance Crisis: Causes and Consequences*. New York: Insurance Information Institute, 2022. https://www.iii.org

- Milliman. *Florida Property Market Trends*. Milliman Research Brief, 2021. https://www.milliman.com

- National Association of Insurance Commissioners (NAIC). *Understanding Moral Hazard and Adverse Selection*. NAIC Consumer Insights Report, 2019. https://content.naic.org

- National Association of Insurance Commissioners (NAIC). *Property/Casualty Insurance Industry Financial Results*. 2022. https://content.naic.org

- National Institute of Building Sciences. *Natural Hazard Mitigation Saves: 2019 Report*. Washington, D.C.: NIBS, 2019. https://www.nibs.org

- National Oceanic and Atmospheric Administration (NOAA). *Historical Hurricane Tracks*; *Sea Level Rise Technical Report*. Washington, D.C.: NOAA, 2022. https://www.noaa.gov

- Pew Charitable Trusts. *Flood-Ready Infrastructure: Challenges and Gaps*. 2020.

Author's Note

By Don D. Brown

As a former legislator, lifelong Floridian, and longtime student of insurance markets, I've seen firsthand how well-intentioned policies can produce unintended — and often devastating — results. This book is not written to assign blame, but to **illuminate choices**. Because every policy decision, every rate cap, every delayed investment, and every act of avoidance comes at a cost — whether we see it or not.

The thesis I've presented is simple, but urgent: **It is cheaper to prepare than to repair.** And it is more honest to fund risk before disaster strikes than to borrow from the future in the aftermath of predictable loss.

This principle isn't ideological — it's actuarial. It's financial. And it's fair.

We owe it to the people of Florida — to our policyholders, our taxpayers, our children — to build a system that recognizes risk, prices it transparently, and encourages behavior that makes us safer. Not just politically safer. **Actually safer.**

I offer this work as a contribution to that cause, and as an invitation to every policymaker, insurer, and citizen willing to ask the hard questions and tell the hard truths — before the next storm arrives.

— **Don D. Brown**
Author and Consultant
Former Member, Florida House of Representatives

About the Author

Don D. Brown is a respected author, consultant, and former legislator with a distinguished career in public policy and insurance reform. A retired insurance agent from DeFuniak Springs, Florida, Brown served on the Walton County Commission, as Republican State Committeeman, Chairman of the Walton County Republican Executive Committee, and as a State Representative in the Florida House of Representatives.

During his eight years in the legislature, Brown became one of Florida's most informed and outspoken voices on insurance and financial issues. Twice recognized by both the Florida Association of Insurance Agents and the Florida Association of Insurance and Financial Advisors, he was known for advocating market-based solutions, smaller government, and principle-driven policymaking. In 2007, he stood nearly alone in opposing HB1A, a massive expansion of government into private insurance markets—objections that time has largely validated.

Brown is the author of numerous books and white papers exploring the intersection of insurance, economics, and public policy, including:

Books

1. *Drowning in Denial: Behavioral Economics and Coastal Insurance Markets: A Path to Resilience* (2024)
2. *Fortifying the Future: Code Plus Standards for Hurricane Resilience and Economic Stability* (2024)

3. *The High Cost of Hidden Risk: Why Florida's Insurance Crisis Can't Be Fixed Without Facing Reality* (2024)
4. *The Capital Drain: How Policy Uncertainty Weakens Catastrophe Insurance Markets* (2024)
5. *Beyond Indemnity: The Evolution, Complexity, and Future of Homeowners Insurance* (2024)
6. *Navigating Uncertainty in Florida's Property Insurance Market: A Strategic Framework for Resilience* (2024)
7. *The 9 Guideline Principles to Enact Change: A Legislator's Memoir — From Outhouse to State House* (2021)
8. *From Roots to Realization: A Journey from the Outhouse to the Statehouse* (2021)
9. *From Roots to Realization: A Legislative Journey* (2021)
10. *Essays on Insurance and Public Policy* (2021)

White Papers

1. *The Importance of Guiding Principles in Public Policymaking*
2. *How Do Other Jurisdictions Manage Hurricane Risk Exposure?*
3. *Parametric Insurance Claims Processing and Smart Contracts on the Blockchain*
4. *Florida's Homeowners Insurance Crisis: A Root Cause Approach with Guiding Principles*
5. *9 Guiding Principles and the "However" Response*
6. *Solving Florida's Homeowners Insurance Crisis: A Strategic Root Cause Analysis* (with Dennis Ross)

7. *Nine Guiding Principles to Enact Change: A Legislator's Journey from Outhouse to Statehouse* (comparative study)

8. *Beyond the Beach Brochure: A Comprehensive Analysis of Florida's Homeowner Insurance Crisis*

Brown continues to write and speak extensively on resilience, insurance markets, and the role of principled policymaking in addressing complex challenges.

Contact Information:

Don D. Brown

PO Box 866

DeFuniak Springs, FL 32435

info@donanddiane.com

www.dondbrown.live

Review Request

The High Cost of Hidden Risk:
Why Florida's Insurance Crisis Can't Be Fixed Without Facing Reality

---

Share Your Thoughts

If you found *The High Cost of Hidden Risk* helpful, I'd be truly grateful if you would consider leaving a short review on Amazon and my website at www.dondbrown.live

Your honest feedback helps other readers and families discover the series — and it supports my mission to create practical, engaging tools that prepare young people to make wise financial decisions.

You don't need to write much — even a sentence or two can make a meaningful difference.

Thank you for being part of this journey!

— Don D. Brown

Made in the USA
Monee, IL
03 November 2026

67381972R00095